Love Revolution

D0885275

Love Revolution

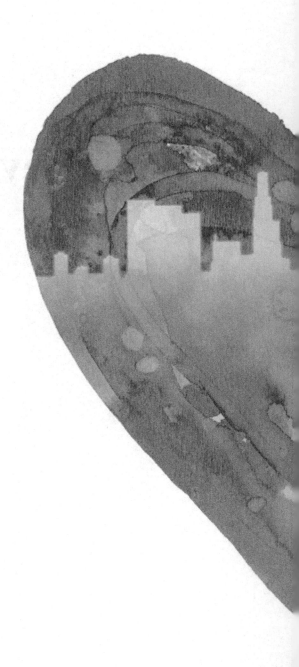

Love Revolution
Stories That Radically Change The Way We Love

Mia Saenz
and
25 Love Revolutionaries

Love Revolution

Stories That Radically Change The Way We Love

ISBN: 978-0-9898852-1-8

Printed in the United States of America
Published by BellaMia Publishing

Cover Design
Creation design: Mia Saenz
Water Color: Whitney Freya
Graphic Artist: Laura Dirzo

Content
Layout, Formatting & Editing: Barry Selby

DEDICATION

This book is dedicated to you.

To you, the ones who have the slightest yearning in your heart to be more in life.

To you who are already on the path of Love - reaching your hand to others to support along life's journey.

To all of you, keep going, growing, and moving forward in love and your inner awareness.

A special thank you to everyone in this book as well as to all those who want to join us on this Love Revolution mission - to love the world one step at a time.

And, my deepest personal thank you to those who have loved me and whom I have loved. My life is richer for it - no matter the outcome.

WITH DEEP GRATITUDE

Starting a Revolution is never easy. When it comes to a Love Revolution it doesn't get any easier. We learned this lesson when we attempted to publish this book initially. I am using the word *attempt* because it was a path with many roadblocks that actually stopped us. It wasn't until we took the reins and responsibility back for this book, that we could move forward.

In so doing, I have the deepest gratitude and love for two of my colleagues and friends (and contributing writers in this book) who stepped up when I couldn't progress any further.

I will always be most grateful to Patty Alfonso who stepped in at a crucial moment, and then entrusting the production of this game-changing book to Barry Selby, who helped us create this beautiful vision in its entirety, allowing us to share it with you.

I am forever in awe of their generous and unconditional love they have shown me and the other writers in this book and movement.

Thank you, Barry and Patty.

A very special thank you to BellaMia Publishing, for taking our book on, when other micro-publishing companies didn't have abilities or skills to handle what was needed. Thankfully, BellaMia came through and delivered the book you have in your hands.

Biggest love,
Mia

Love Revolution

Love Revolution

CONTENTS

PREFACE

From a very young age, I was aware of my ability to love and my deep compassion for others. I didn't fully understand the depth or importance of this until I was older.

As humans, we have been kept down in shame and dysfunction. We don't fully understand it until we begin to feel the pain, that our entire framework of life falls off kilter. We are taught to put others first before ourselves. It's backward! Each person has a soul and each soul has its own calling and own path to living. The world and life are changing. A new revolution of love has begun.

Welcome to Love Revolution.

Love Revolution is a vast movement that began at each and every birth. This movement of love contains within it freedom, peace, consistency, and empowering grace.

I became a Love Coach because it was my life's mission. Most people think I am a relationship coach, and in some ways I am an inner personal relationship coach. To build the inner workings and dust off the cobwebs is the most courageous act one can accomplish. There is no bigger challenge than to shift from the wounded soul and heart to the victorious person you were created to be. As this is accomplished, a new world opens up before you.

In my younger years, what I saw was not the image I see before me today. Growing up the youngest of four (five if you count my twin who died forcing my birth at six months), life was difficult, hard, sad with speckles of happiness. I grew up being quite reserved, introverted and extremely shy. My priority was serving others and not myself. This looked like most women and caregivers who go to bed at night without thinking of themselves or their needs that day. Women who are constantly dreaming of the day everything will feel balanced, and life will be "theirs."

That day has now come. That day you have been looking for, for many years, it's finally here and now it's time for you to open the door and step through.

Self-love is not self-care. Self-care is an aspect of self-love. Self-love is deeper and richer on a conscious awareness level. Self-love is the depths of love one dives into. It is the relationship between you and your higher power. Many call this higher power, God. The name used to represent God doesn't matter. There are many languages, religions, and thought processes about this higher power, so the name is not as important as your faith in knowing.

We teach and preach what we most need to stir our life into the path we most desire to learn. When one understands and lives a life of love, the outcome is vast. Everything in life begins to ripple out in a positive manner to fully support us instead of hinder us. As humanity grows their love muscle, there will be a larger and expanding awareness of respect and love for one another. We will begin to honor each other's journey as deeply as we honor our own. Wars will cease, borders will crumble, separate and divisive governments will no longer exist, and we will become one government of the people, one nation with states that were once individual countries.

Just as everything takes time to understand and to grow into, the vision described above will also take time. It will be perhaps even five to seven centuries before conscious awareness is global. Will we as a species be here to exist and express that? This is a choice we make within our core center.

This is the choice for Love Revolution.

Each day allows us to begin anew. Each moment supports our choices and commitments. This is our moment in time, our glory and our time of awareness that this life is mine and I will live it in love.

Celebrations in life come when you see your world in the rainbow spectrum of love.

In this book, you will find diverse and empowering chapters from key experts, coaches and speakers all on a mission to empower others and YOU, in your own Love Revolution. Take time to open your heart, listen, and apply what you learn here. Then, take time to find out more about the contributing authors by visiting their websites for more information. As you embrace this Love Revolution, may you find your own love.

With Love,
Mia Saenz

Founder of *Love Revolution*
Self Love Teacher
Founder and Editor in Chief of *BellaMia Magazine*
Love Mastery, Inner Personal Growth into Self Love Program

Love Revolution

Loves Changes The Energy Of Your Story

"And, in the end, the love you take is equal to the love you make."
~ The Beatles

What I'm about to tell you, you may have never heard before. I want you to allow it to absorb into your very being.

You are a *miracle*!

You are deeply loved!

You are not alone!

These are the truest words you will ever hear! They are truer than most people will ever realize.

We all feel alone, unheard, as if no one else can feel or reach our pain. This is simply not the truth, not about you or me or anyone.

Our beliefs begin to form from the moment we are born and this is when our understanding is shaped.

MY BEGINNING

I have early memories that are mine and I have memories as they were told to me. I never questioned that my mom or dad loved me but looking now through adult eyes, there was no peace or stillness in my childhood.

My mother and father began their love affair two and a half years before I was born, each married to another. They couldn't stay apart. I was born an illegitimate child and told my twin sister died forcing my birth in the sixth month of the pregnancy. My father was twenty years older than my mother and he was Latin. When I was a child, being Mexican or in my case, half Mexican taught me about the world of discrimination. I am light skinned with brown hair and I don't look ethnic. Although my physical features resemble my siblings, my coloring is somewhat different than my blonde-haired, blue-eyed older sister or that of my green-eyed brothers.

Being the youngest, and my father's only natural child, my mother used me as a pawn to get his attention. My mother was abusive: mentally, physically and emotionally. Even in that abuse, I never questioned that she loved me - I knew she did. I wouldn't understand until I was an adult that my mother suffered from mental illness.

She and my father had a tumultuous relationship that my mom used to describe as "Star-Crossed Lovers." They couldn't live with each other and they couldn't live without each other.

Love Revolution

My first memory of physical abuse happened when I was four years old. I was awakened early, around six in the morning. My mother pulled me out of a deep sleep and told me I needed to run after my father and stop him, bring him back home before he went to work. They had been fighting, again.

I ran from my room, out of the house and down the street trying to stop my daddy driving away in his car, but he didn't see me. I ran and ran until his car turned the corner out of sight. I remember how cold the sidewalk was on my bare feet and how my pink and white gingham print babydoll nightgown was so thin. I remember I was cold.

I returned to the house to tell my mom I didn't catch daddy. What happened next was beyond explanation, especially for a four-year old. My mother completely flipped out. She woke up my brothers and sister and just went completely crazy.

She made me lie down on the floor in the bedroom I shared with my sibling. She directed my two brothers and sister to stand, one at my head and one on each side of me while she stood at my feet. We looked like a cross with my mother and the other little children spread around me. She began to spank me and commanded them to do the same.

During this dark moment in my life, I recall my sister saying, "I don't want to hit my baby sister!" I have no idea where this came from, but I told her, "You have to hit me or she will hit you." When the episode was finished, I was shut away in the closet until she decided to let me out.

This experience would be traumatic for anyone, especially a small child. I didn't share it with you to have you be consumed with feeling bad for me. I have worked through all the issues suffered in my childhood traumas. What I want you to take away from my sharing of this experience, is that we can all teach ourselves what true love is. We can each learn how to build and develop our emotional intelligence levels in order to thrive in this life. I have become a 'thriver,' not a survivor.

This is one of the many incidents that make up my history. Along with the dysfunction of my mother, I experienced a five-year stretch where my girl scout leader's husband molested me several times a month. It began when I was six years old and I stopped it the summer I turned eleven.

My trauma isn't unique, although in the era I grew up in, this kind of stuff was not talked about or shared publicly. People suffered in silence.

I am grateful my life has given me compassion and a stance from that very young age, to be a voice for others. I became the Love Activist that I am now.

One of the symptoms of having trauma is Post-Traumatic Stress Disorder. I have PTSD. My life's journey took me to a place where I got help with it. The PSTD was triggered by the "9/11" event. It would be the beginning of my healing journey and my coming alive, my return to love.

My PTSD became increasingly worse after 9/11. I was unable to stop crying or to even care properly for my children. The stress of dealing with my PTSD pushed my first husband to his limits, as he had to now take care of the children. This aggravation increased daily until one day, he lost it. We both did. His anger had risen to an all-time high and one day he broke down my bedroom door. It frightened me so much that I had a psychotic break. I didn't know that I was also bi-polar at the time and I reverted back to that small four-year-old child in the closet: hurt, lost, confused and in pain. I could share the dramatic and tragic details of that day, but they aren't important.

What is important to know here, is that there is help. You can learn deep love for yourself, something most of us have not been taught. You can come from the darkness into the light and create a life that is supportive and loving to, for, and of you.

In this space of being broken down in fear – I survived. Six months later it took me to a place that would be the beginning of my transformation. I went willingly to the Meadows in Wickenburg,

Arizona, a very beautiful open and outdoor treatment facility that provides help for depression. This was a place where celebrities and other people with financial means came in order to get over all types of addiction. This was my deep learning ground, my place to discover who I truly was.

Since I didn't have an addiction, I got to experience everyone else's twelve step meetings. I chose a different one each night. I really learned in those five weeks how everything is related to my experience. I could see my mom's drug addiction that caused my premature birth. I could see how alcohol affects not just the body but the entirety of families. I went to about eight different twelve step meetings and revisited them often because I really wanted to understand everything. I found this process fascinating. Who knew it would crack me open like a walnut and turn me onto a path of recovery? Recovery from fear, from the lack of knowing who I was and finally, to discovering who I truly am - magnificent. This was the beginning of my integration into my own journey.

The first time I was told I was a miracle, I did what I always did; I deflected it off to everyone. My standard reply was, "We are all miracles, not just me."

During my stay at the Meadows, the head of the facility would come into my group therapy sessions every day to look at me and say to me, "Mia, do you know you are a *miracle*"?

I would answer the same each time, "Everybody is." She would respond every time, "Yes, but do YOU realize you are a *miracle*?" She listened to my reply each day and then she would leave.

She came and went like a light breeze for 35 days. This was literally God's gift to me. I didn't know it at the time, but it got me thinking. I knew she had read all about me and the severe childhood I had. I recall one of the psychiatrists stating that with such a traumatic childhood, it was a miracle that my siblings and I should be alive today. That severity of abuse that we endured, didn't usually keep a child safe, let alone alive. We were the lucky ones.

I knew when the head of the Meadows would come in and tell me I was a miracle, she was revealing something to me: my true inner being. How did I know this? I don't know, I simply did.

You see, when I was young I developed my own, very special relationship with God. I would talk to God to find comfort and answers. I became a good listener. I found a great calmness when I would ask for guidance. I believe those who claim they cannot hear God's answers to their questions have not learned to listen.

As a very lonely child in a household of six, I built a strong relationship with my God. It is, I believe, in the end, what saved my life.

I began to look at what a miracle felt like, what it would look like and to see how it related to me. I realized it had to do with consciously being aware of who I truly was.

Little did I know at that point in my life, that in seven years I would come alive and teach the world what I came to know was my heart's true desire.

This is what self-reflection looks like and how we can make those shifts within ourselves. That which once kept me down and trapped was now released by consciously developing this love affair with myself.

Everything we say, hear and listen to is absorbed into our bodies and becomes a part of our mental awareness. This is where we have the choice to believe or not believe what we are hearing: to accept or decline the messages.

This is where our human journey can shift into having the power to create a life that is free of judgment, limitation and fear. Believe what your soul is telling you to believe, just be sure it is your soul talking and not the beliefs that others have forced you to believe. Become a clear thinker.

This is a life - shifting experience!

As we do this inner self-growth work, we become clear about our own thoughts and those that come from the programming of others.

Love Revolution

Know you are not alone. We all go through difficulties, maybe not severe trauma but certainly self-doubt and questioning. Everything that our parents, relatives, church, governments, media, teachers and even our friends and friends' parents tell us when we are young, forms our belief systems.

When we do this self-love work on a conscious level, we change. Self-care is not the same as self-love - it is the beginning stage of learning what is important. Self-love is the deep, conscious aspect that shifts our thinking, our belief systems and brings us to a place of awareness and self-responsibility.

What happens? Shame is removed. Your value is recognized. Love appears where there once was hatred and the evolution of your emotional intelligence grows. We become whole! No more fragmented pieces and no more fears that hold or bind you to something that was not your choice.

This is what true freedom looks like: you creating a life you love and changing the energy of your story.

I would like to share a few tools that can help you move into a higher level of self-growth.

This type of growth is all about self-reflection, self-responsibility, and self-love.

Please know my website is a resource for you to visit and download any tools that are there for free.

"Dream. Believe. Create." is the process that allows you to expand your awareness of what you truly desire in your life. Here is how it works:

- Find a quiet place in order to begin your relaxed meditative/dream state.

- Have a notebook to take notes.

- Look at your life as if you were creating a movie.

- Create in your imagination (visionary work), the most exciting experience you want to have.

- Consider these five pillars: spiritual, body, work, relationships and home.

- Dream big to the point that you want it so much that you can believe you can be it, then go create it.

Literally, when you take footsteps forward, a path is created to what you are seeking and your answers will appear.

Now, for the tip of your lifetime…

If you are still depressed and staying in that lower energy, guess what? Nothing will happen! You need to raise your energy levels up (energy otherwise known as your vibration). Understand that love and God vibrate on the same level. This means when you raise your energy, your vibration, you are opening up to all that is for you.

Another tip is gratitude. Gratitude is the fastest way to get back into that state of grace where you are higher with your energy and you are connected to your life and dreams.

"Mirror Work" is one practice that is vital to each individual opening up and connecting to their own self-love. "Mirror Work" is the practice of looking into the mirror and working with a quality, question or reflection. In this context, this practice is when you look in the mirror and say "I love you." If you cannot tell yourself "I love you" without consequence, then you are not in a space of inner awareness. Unfortunately, most people are repulsed or feel a disconnect when they look into the mirror and say "I love you." If you are experiencing any disconnect or negative ideations when doing "Mirror Work," do not give up. Keep at it and ask for help. We are here to assist by email and/or appointments. I share this with you so you understand that you are not alone and that there is help. (See directions on my website for a three-part video series sharing details. You can download for free at www.miasaenz.com).

What all this self-growth work does, is connect us to our own love. As we grow in life and our belief systems, we tend to disconnect from our inner love and our bodies. This consciousness work that we do, is self-love (not self-care) that connects us to who we truly are. These are stages of the reflection work.

Healing the inner child is primary to gain one's emotional intelligence. We are full of emotions and often allow them to lead our decision making in every situation. Self-love and doing the inner child work develops the area of the human psyche that once had no guidance, only self-depravation (see three-part video series for the directions).

The "Inner Child" work I teach is done through a process of a guided meditation to meet your younger self and heal all the wounds that were left raw and unhealed or that felt abandoned and unloved. This is powerful work and it will change the energy of your story through love.

Most of us have not been taught to love ourselves. We go into this inner self-growth healing work to understand our own self-love. We must understand that to succeed, we need to use the power of our intention for making a change, in order to even begin to see a change. This is what true transformation is about.

We must learn to love ourselves the way we would love our own babies; with beauty and glory and magnificence. When was the last time you felt completely loved from the inside out? This is not a judgment but an awareness.

This is the most beautiful gift one can give themselves. I even equate it to the best travel adventure you will ever take in your lifetime.

Getting to understand, know and love yourself is the greatest gift of all.

What we are told or believe creates who and what we think about ourselves. Until that day when you decide to break all the barriers, to not believe everything that was once told to you, you will remain trapped inside of you. Taking action now, making love a lifestyle change, is what will CHANGE YOUR LIFE!

Love well!
Mia Saenz

Love Revolution

What's Love Got To Do With It?

"Those who fail to learn from their history, are doomed to repeat it.
~ George Santayana

I am a relationship attraction expert, helping strong successful women create and find balance in life, love and business. I am also a passionate champion for the divine feminine.

That is my formal introduction when asked. However, I wasn't born this way, and I certainly didn't start life with masterful relationship skills! Did you?

Like most people, I have had a less than perfect journey with love and relationships, especially in my youth. To illustrate and educate, here are two themes that governed a lot of my relationship history – "Perfect Love" and "Avoiding the Macho."

PERFECT LOVE

I was naive, like most. I made a lot of mistakes, that's for sure. Relationship and love were not an easy road for me. When I first began my dating adventures, I made a lot of mistakes!

I was inept and clumsy in my early romance and courtship "experiments." I hadn't read any books or taken classes back then. I was clueless about matters of love and romance. Of course, you can't relate. Despite my lack of knowledge and skill, I did enjoy some exciting and romantic (though short-lived) relationships.

In my late teens and early twenties, each relationship I entered, would abruptly end, with alarming regularity. It didn't help that I would be the one breaking up with my partner every time. After the initial chemistry and passion, things would change. At some point in the first few months, she and I would have an upset of some sort, which would lead to an argument. At that time, I would call it quits and leave. This happened repeatedly, with several women.

That is, until I learned a powerful lesson. But I'm getting ahead of myself.

A little history: I was born and raised in England, grew up in a small, stoic Jewish family governed by the loving parents of two boys. Life at home was usually peaceful, somewhat reserved and "nice." My parents' relationship was stable and calm. And, to the best of my memory, they never argued in front of me and my brother.

During my formative years (up until around 7 or 8), just like everyone else, my beliefs about life, and particularly about love and relationships, began to solidify. I watched what my parents did and said in their relationship as the model of how life and love work.

I was absorbing what I witnessed and experienced as the way life and love happened. My parents unwittingly and unconsciously impressed upon me a lot of beliefs, including a key teaching that when you are loving, you never argue, you don't get upset. This is what they showed me, and this is what I subconsciously learned to believe.

It became a key belief for me: Arguments and love do not mix.

I lived this rule automatically and unconsciously. According to my belief, arguments marked the end of love, which coincided with the end of the relationship. This played out in all my early relationships. Each relationship would start with love, and end with or because of an argument, every single time. In my mind, that argument could only happen because there was no love left. I believed my only path was to leave. Of course, I didn't know I was living by that rule at the time. And in hindsight, I know this was a mistake in approach. I, for sure, had no idea I was missing out on the pleasure of make-up sex!

20/20 HINDSIGHT

In case you didn't realize this, none of us are born with user manuals, and our parents didn't have an instruction book or training on how to raise us. Our early orientation and learning about life comes from experience. We learn how the world works by absorbing everything we see, hear, taste, and touch, like a sponge. Our subconscious mind is that sponge, soaking up everything we experience and storing it as the "rules of life."

Our young subconscious minds learn about health (what to eat, what not to eat), about money (what bills get paid, what doesn't get paid), about love, about other people, how we treat each other, how relationship works, and a lot more. We learn all this by observing our parents, and other adults around us. We learn by imitation; we copy what we see them doing. It's how we learn. This becomes our default programming and installed belief system.

At age six or seven, our conscious mind takes over. This is the gatekeeper for our mind, controlling what we learn. It controls what we take in, and also governs what choices we make.

However, our subconscious mind has already been programmed with several years of learning about life, automatically. This runs our default beliefs and choices, automatically, and is particularly relevant when it comes to our relationships.

If your family expressed itself with a lot of shouting and yelling, you probably learned to express love that way and recognize love as being loudly expressed. Yes, for you, love is only recognized when it is loud and shouted!

Perhaps you were raised in an abusive environment, whether it was emotional, mental, physical, or even sexual abuse. This experience would reflect and influence your adult relationships, as you will tend to attract abusive partners to feel abused, or you may be the abuser with your partner. You enter a new relationship with somebody you think is wonderful and perfect, and three months or three weeks into the relationship, you begin experiencing something familiar - some form of abuse.

You will repeat these imprinted childhood patterns, whether these patterns involve abuse, addiction, abandonment, or something else. You are unwittingly (or rather unconsciously) drawn to partners who will uphold the patterns you learned as a child, automatically. Whatever relationship programming and love patterns you carry from childhood, they will play out in your adult relationships. Basically your adult relationship choices are controlled by how you were raised. This is how most of us function in relationship.

But wait, there's more!

One of the biggest collective subconscious beliefs we learn (falsely) is that love comes from others. We are not enough unless we are loved by someone else. This codependent rule pervades our society and most relationships. It is a metaphorical plague in our culture – almost every love song and romance movie from the past fifty plus years tells us love is outside of us, that we can't live without someone else's love.

All of this is a lie! It is codependent propaganda!

There is good news, though. These patterns and automatic programs will stop, when we awaken and begin to change.

One way we can start the process of rewiring and rewriting our old beliefs, is to learn (and remember) to love ourselves again. Many of us have forgotten to consciously love ourselves. Which is why I frequently teach this to my clients. And why I have a gift for you:

SELF-LOVE HEARTWORK PRACTICE

As I mentioned, many of us are falsely programmed to believe that love comes from someone else. We fall in love with someone, they love us, and we feel great. They stop loving us, we feel awful. Like a ping-pong ball, we are at the mercy of love. Love happens to us, rather than us loving ourselves first, filling ourselves up with our own love.

My invitation, my gift to you, is intended to help you have healthier relationships, beginning with yourself. This practice may appear deceptively simple. However, you will discover it delivers a powerful transformation. This is a slimmed down version of my full guided meditation practice that includes audio meditations and deeper exploration.

This Self-Love Mirror Meditation Practice is simple to do, however it may not be easy to fully embrace, initially. It takes willingness, vulnerability and openness.

HOW:

- Stand or sit in front of a mirror.

- Put your hand on your heart.

- Breathe slowly and deeply, bringing yourself into the present moment.

- Let the world around you stop. Look in the mirror, into your own eyes.

- Out loud, from your heart, say "I love you" into your own eyes in the mirror. Or if you prefer, say, "I love me" into your own eyes in the mirror.

- Intend to feel this love coming from you and coming to you.

- Do this for a minimum of five minutes, once in the morning, and once again in the evening.

This is for you, not for anyone else, just for you. I invite you to commit to do this practice every day, for at least 30 days. In just 30 days, your life will be transformed. You will know you are loved, that you deserve love, and it begins with filling your heart first.

AVOIDING THE MACHO

I spent most of my high school years being bullied by other boys. I became very reserved and shy. I barely participated in sports or social activities. Being macho was definitely not in my comfort zone. During my teen years, I wasn't the jock or player; girls didn't fall in love with me. Girls did seek me out though. I was the boy they trusted, the boy they confided in. They could cry on my shoulder. I was the nice guy. It was a badge of honor somehow. I felt respected by the girls. Even if I didn't get to date any of them!

I was averse to being macho for sure, especially after watching that behavior among my teen peers and adversaries.

Fast forward into adulthood: I have always been attracted to strong, successful women. Some women I dated earned more than I did, some even had nicer cars than I did. Dating them, I was the nice guy. I would do anything for them. I never took control away from them.

The sex was great, and it was fun. Even in sex, they took charge and I happily enjoyed being the recipient. I didn't realize I was choosing women who were more in their masculine alpha countenance than I was. Hindsight is helpful at times.

I thought to be a real man meant being a macho bully, to be in control, to be tougher than any other man, to be self-centered and ego-centric. I didn't want this, and that aversion drove me to dive deep into my life-long exploration of self-discovery and personal growth. For more than three decades so far, I have explored and studied human awareness and development, and grown in my own spiritual practice. I have achieved a Master's Degree in Spiritual Psychology, and earned a professional license as a spiritual counselor and practitioner.

Throughout this journey, I was becoming more uneasy with the archetype of the macho man in the world. I didn't align with the role of being an alpha male, which to me meant a tough and unemotional man. In fact, this reached a peak after my last bad breakup at the end of 2006.

This was the third relationship in a row where the same experience happened, the same pattern had played out. It was clear – this was about me, not them. In spite of all the training, education and experiential learning I had under my belt, I still didn't know what I was doing wrong. Sometimes we are so close to our issues, we don't see what they are. I prayed for guidance.

Thankfully, a few months later, my prayer was answered. I was exposed to perhaps the most important learning experience of my life. I dived deep into this life-changing understanding and embodiment of the profoundly powerful dance of masculine and feminine polarity.

This deeper adventure began in 2007, and provided me an understanding of the masculine and feminine polarity in love, in relationship, in life. I have had the privilege of studying with some giants in this field, including Satyen & Suzanne Raja (WarriorSage), David Deida, Alison Armstrong and John Gray.

This immersion and continued embodiment has changed my life, opened me to my inner guidance and evolved my view of the world, and continues to this day.

Embracing and honoring my true Masculine nature consciously for the first time was an epiphany. I know the macho is a creation of the ego, not a true authentic expression. I also know why that never worked for me. I was happy to release it.

Now, as a open-hearted and deeply masculine man, I live aligned to my authentic nature and integrity, aware of my true strength and authority, and know why I am here.

This awareness and self-knowledge undergirds and inspires my life and my calling in the world. My coaching and message are birthed from this understanding. It guides my life, my calling and my service to women, to the Divine Feminine, and to my clients.

THE WAY OF THE DIVINE FEMININE

Who I am has evolved through this decades-long journey. In my own work, I embody, express and share a rich blend of teachings that speak to the authentic nature and power of the masculine/feminine paradigm.

I am deeply humbled by the majesty of the divine Feminine. She is awe-inspiring and magnificent. Over the past decade I have experienced thousands of women recognizing, embracing and embodying their true and authentic femininity. I have been inspired on so many levels, and it has called forth my true vocation in the world. When women access and embrace their Feminine authority, they blossom and open to who they really are. These women embody a much deeper flow and connection to life, and they express a graceful way of being. This is a paradigm shift for many women, and for many men also, including me. I believe, as women embody their Divine Feminine, this energy and perspective improves their emotional, mental and physical health, their connection to Spirit, and their innate expression and wholeness. This paradigm shift will also change the planet.

In my studies and observation, I have witnessed the Goddess movement, which helps women learn to connect to their deeper core values, to shed their masculine roles and behaviors (at least for a moment) and to discover sisterhood and connection to nature and

Spirit. All of this is magnificent. Yet, I feel it is a stepping stone to something even more potent and freeing for women.

Beyond the Goddess, I feel women are being called to step into a more powerful and profound role on this planet, as the Divine Feminine. I have come to recognize the Divine Feminine embodies three elements. The true power of the Feminine is a blend of the *Priestess* (divinity and spiritual guidance), the *Queen* (majesty, benevolence and caring authority), and the *Warrior* (focused power and strength). These three elements are within every woman.

YOU ARE VITAL FOR THE WORLD'S HEALTH

Ladies, this is my invitation to you. You are opening to and owning your feminine power and divine authority. You will discover your ownership will restore your full expression. When you embody your feminine fullness, you accept and embrace your true strength, majesty, grace, and responsibility. You get things done, and in relationship you also enjoy your man leading and taking care of you as an equal partner. You take care of yourself. It is your full expression of this divine feminine authority which inspires your powerful relationship, as well as your life and your calling.

Being deeply immersed in this masculine/feminine conversation and embracing and owning my own masculine heart and purposeful expression, I have become deeply passionate about supporting and guiding women to attract amazing relationships. I humbly serve strong, successful women with two primary transformations.

First, I help them heal their past, their hurts and heart-breaks, so they become whole once again. This includes realigning and updating their subconscious memories of childhood experience, freeing them from their history (or is that *herstory*?).

Second, I am dedicated to helping women remember, respect and own their divine feminine authority. I am discovering more and more my calling to help these same women find balance in their lives, outside relationships, and truly to become a feminine power on the planet.

For a long time, men (of the macho persuasion) have run the world as a generally patriarchal society. Men have really done a number on the planet and our culture, including how women have been mistreated. This is becoming more visible thanks to the #metoo movement and new conversations.

I believe it is time for true feminine authority and matriarchal leadership to take its place up front.

My work and message are evolving. I speak about this topic frequently online (both written and in my video livestreams) and in person. Women are listening more now. I love speaking to this receptivity.

As women embody this, I am inspired. Assisting women to own their authentic feminine power is fulfilling to my heart. As you step into true leadership in the world from a feminine heart, everything changes for the better.

It is why I love what I do! And why I am a passionate champion for the Divine Feminine.

PB&J
Barry Selby

Born To Break It

"Greatness has to break the gravity of its environment."
~ TD Jakes

Somewhere outside my bedroom door, under the waning super moon, a mama cat sings a diaphanous, "NO," unraveling her protest note by note, and spinning it like yarn into the crisp night air. Deep inside my belly, a lightning bolt tipped like an arrow strikes the ground.

I am transported to another time, some 11 years ago, and to another "NO" lingering in the air.

I am in the oddest of places, an evangelical church in Phoenix, Arizona. I say "oddest" because I grew up in these churches and long ago buried any desire to be in their company. But heaven knows I am in need of a reconciliation with GOD. I have also fallen in love with a Christian man and my desire for him has compelled me to try this again.

God uses what works. Remember that.

The needed reconciliation: My mother, while participating in an evangelical prison ministry, was brutally murdered in 1997 just 18 months after my father died and only one week before my wedding.

On this fateful morning, I still blame her god.

FOR.

EVERYTHING.

At this church service, in the city of the flaming bird, I have heard the pastor say something important. I have also just arrived at the altar with my child in front of me, looking confused at the way I snatched her up from the pew. I am baptizing her in my tears and in the sound of my voice:

"Not on my watch! Not my daughter! The oppression and the violation stop at my back. She will walk free of it!"

I am watching a dense, ugly cloud of spirit matter stall out behind me as my tears roll down my face, each a pearly offering.

Just like I commanded, not one molecule of this terrorizing presence is able to come through me or around me. It cannot penetrate the boundary of my words. And it never does. As I listen to mama cat serenade the night sky, my daughter is nearly 19 years old and the boundary of my words is holding firm. I said she would walk free of it and free she walks.

On another occasion, in this same church, I ask Jesus to let me continue his healing ministry on earth through my hands and then I ask him to show me the feminine face of God. He does, but not there.

Goodbye church. Goodbye Christian man. Goodbye Phoenix.

By the sinuous sound of mama cat's song, I am transported again, much further back in time.

I am standing at another altar. I am about 12 or 13. A preacher has his hand on my forehead. He has just pronounced that one day I will be a mighty witness for God. I hear his words, feel his touch, and lose consciousness, literally and figuratively.

That moment, that touch, that pronouncement all seem, in retrospect, to have formed a giant portal into destruction. By the time I was 16, the preacher man's words seemed long gone. I was hooked on methamphetamines and was being inducted into a world of horrors no 16 year old should ever face.

It's no mystery to me what happened. To be a mighty witness for God implies a miracle. In turn, miracles require a bit of tension in the story, a tragedy in the third act, something from which one can be raised as though from the dead. But most importantly, a miracle requires understanding.

You cannot heal what you do not understand so deeply that you have breathed it, mixed with oxygen, just as necessary as air.

You cannot break the hold of something that has never sustained you.

Degradation, Drug Addition, Perilous "Love," Craven Desire...

These things are all the dual sustainers and destroyers of life when your insides are crumpled and broken and when God is long forgotten.

Long forgotten...

As I write to you now, I am sitting in Guanajuato, the capital city of Guanajuato, Mexico (another desert landscape) in front of a broken window (the portal through which my house was robbed last summer). In its brokenness rests the entirety of my testimony. It is the latest altar in my life, my daily reminder of who God really is. It holds that promised miracle, my rise from the ashes of my burning times. In it rests the track of my destiny.

This particular window, like my once crumpled and broken insides, is a vulnerable place in an otherwise secure property. The cut in the glass forms a partial Vesica Piscis, the central part of a Venn diagram that represents the overlap of two things. A line runs to and from it as though it is possible to exit one Venn diagram and enter another.

Within this suggested movement from one overlapping set of realities to another lies the truth of salvation. This is all I need to understand and to transmit into this world. It is all I need to bring alive in my clients as they heal and as they lay claim to their dreams:

In trauma and exploitation, your vulnerability overlaps with someone else's desire to use you, loot your resources, violate your body. You name it, they will use your vulnerability to do it.

But God…

> *"My grace is sufficient for you, for my power is made perfect in weakness."*
> *~ 2 Corinthians 12:9*

In other words, God enters the opening formed by your vulnerability in order to touch you, to perfect the Divine work, to commune. The Venn diagram constructed in this overlap of God with your weakness is perfection. Within this rapturous space, a new path (constructed of God's passionate devotion for you) unfolds like a waveform. The wild gyrations of this serpentine path are the aftershocks of implantation.

God always enters with a dream!

Eventually, if you stay in this overlapping space, and if you cleave to the unruly path, the arrow of your intentions comes into full alignment with your dream and the sufficiency of the grace that inspired it. Finally, the wild, dynamic movement of the path snaps into a straight line. That line is then laid down like an arrow-tipped lightning strike in the track of your destiny. The very next time your mouth opens, destiny's words leap out.

In that last paragraph, I have just described for you the ultimate Love Revolution. Its name is "Faith." It refuses to accept things at face value, instead calling up and calling forth "the substance of things hoped for, the evidence of things not seen" (Hebrews 11:1). Faith trusts and then manifests the Divine Promise implanted in your spirit womb. It adheres to that promise no matter what your eyes see.

Words are Faith's vessels.

Two words leap out at me from the beginning of this story: "Diaphanous NO."

Many years ago, I had a vision that I would be a midwife to other people's dreams. In a subsequent vision, I saw that I would go on a long journey during which time I would say "NO" a lot. At the end of that long journey, I understood that all of my dreams would come true.

To become The Dream Midwife™ appeared at that time to be my only aspiration. But I had another dream, hidden, buried in the folds of its many twists and turns.

I wanted to be loved.

The things against which I would have to apply that word, "NO" were the many siren songs of perilous "love" that have, over the years, arrived to insert themselves as false idols obscuring the true face of Divinity, hiding my own true face, and blocking my way. In the repetitive act of rebuking these malformed narratives, my dreams are continuously being born, and with them, the many dreams I have been called to catch in the birthing hour.

That explains the "NO," but what about "diaphanous?"

It means "transparent" and "ethereal." A dense "NO" obscures. It forms a mask over the speaker. A diaphanous "NO," makes the speaker, and the source of the speaker's power, visible for all to see. In its ethereal expression the speaker's true identity can be known and another word formed:

YES!

And in the forming of this new word, the bonds of a crippled life can be broken and left behind as beauty overtakes the ashen dust of yesterday and reforms tomorrow in the image of God.

Which, with the fading of the mama cat's cry and the arrival of the morning sunrise, returns me to the promise held in the hands of the old man preacher I met that day so long ago. Very simply put, there has never really been a false step in my life. Every tragedy and every triumph have contained the truth of my life sentence just as he called it.

I was…

Born to Break It.

I am here to help you do the same.

Rebecka Eggers

Love: The Strategic Advantage™

"Learning to use love's power is the single most important criteria to a happy loved filled life."
~ Kimberley Heart

Our time is running out! You know that; you sense it in your bones and in your heart. Consequently, many are scrambling to stop the world from crumbling. I say, stop trying to resuscitate a dead corpse. We should do nothing to save what has stopped serving us. Let the old ways and the old world die!

If you need convincing that the old ways don't work, let me remind you of what you know. Almost fifty percent of marriages end in divorce or in separation. What this figure does not address is how many people stay in loveless marriages or continue to cohabitate.

I do not want to address your personal love life, but rather your business loveless life. This may seem strange in an anthology of love in the modern age, until you really dig down and think about it. You spend about half of your waking day at work. For many of us, it's much more than that. Yet, in the environment where we spend most of our waking time, there is little or no love. Think about it, how does your philosophy of life and love sync with your workday?

I am not talking about affairs in the work place. I'm speaking about one of the most powerful tools of creation that we have – love. When love is missing from the workplace, the consequences are extreme. There is a lack of vision, a collapsing of imagination, a lack of belonging with dignity, a lack of compassion. Dogma becomes the name of the game, rather than dialogue, and there is a dearth of dreams, and the waning of wisdom. This not only hurts a company's bottom line, it hurts you on more levels than you realize.

More than thirty years as the chief advisor to captains of industry has taught me that those who are truly successful bring love into the workplace. For the heads of law firms and corporations who seek me out, I imbue love into every solution. I just never use the word.

I readily admit that most leaders who have infused their work place with the essence of love don't conceptualize it as that. Why? Because too often they don't really know that what they are doing is called "love." They know it works, but they have yet to identify that the power to create, manifest, and add to their success is based in a solid foundation of love.

Love is not an abstract noun. It's more than a philosopher's definition. It's a power, a strength, a talent, the beginning-and-end of what we say we want in life. The power of love has been hijacked because of our mono-vision about what it is. We have very few words for love in all its flavors and intricacies.

What an insult to humankind, that arguably the most important power we have—love—is denigrated to a very few words. Can you come up with ten words for love? I found 142 different words for coffee, I counted 67 words for a car in one thesaurus. For shoes, I counted 73 before my eyes began to cross. The few adjectives that stand for love are so without the essence of its power that it's no wonder we have never considered it an important part of the work environment, even if we're among the few who have seen it work in our businesses.

Let's make love real and practical. As I review love's intricacies, keep in mind that I'm talking about the workplace. You can and should translate this to your personal life, but for now focus on your loveless work environment.

Love is about giving of your knowledge, your strengths, your power, and your wisdom. In addition, it's about giving in the way that the other person can receive what you offer.

It is about responding to the other people in the work environment in such a way that they know they've been heard and appreciated. Even if you don't agree, you honor the idea that their thoughts and feelings are worthy. Responding is about honoring yourself and the other person.

Love is about respecting. Respecting means taking into consideration the other person's emotional nature. For some of us that would mean speaking to us in a clear, concise, get-to-the-point manner. For others, that would mean easing into a conversation and then sandwiching the news by saying something nice, communicating what you came to share, and then saying something nice.

Love is about taking the time to know the people around you, to know the depth and breadth of the business, the depth and breadth of your function in the business. It's much more than understanding – it is to integrate your understanding so that it becomes a part of who you are. Truly valuable people in the workplace, whether they are employees or leaders, know their functions at this level.

Love is about having the humility to be intimate. Humility is allowing each day to be new and not being imprisoned by how it has "always been." Intimacy means being open, close, vulnerable and trusting. When we use the word "intimacy" we almost always think about our interpersonal relationships. It is imperative in the work environment that we are intimate with our work. Be open to it, be close to it, be vulnerable and take risks. Trust yourself and the outcome of what you are producing.

So how can you be vulnerable with a project? Vulnerability means to be changed by what you're doing, risk the pain of failure, and for some even more frighteningly, risk success. Be willing to trust yourself, those you work with, and the business, in order to propel you to the next level of your own development.

Commitment is an integral part of love in the work environment. Taking a stand, moving ahead when it is not easy to do so, stopping and re-evaluating when there are too many road blocks and an unrelenting pursuit to the goal. And more importantly, how you achieve that goal. All of these processes involve true commitment.

Caring about what you do, how you do it, and who you do it with is also part of love in the workplace. Excellence is born of caring.

Imagine with me. You go to work every day to a place that is filled with giving, and responding, where respect is an everyday way of life, a place where you move beyond understanding to knowing. Here everyone allows you to be human and make errors, not hold you as the "person who screws up." Imagine a place where people are open, and where you feel close to others. Imagine it is safe enough to risk being vulnerable and to trust. In that environment how would your life change? What would happen to your creativity level? What would happen to your productivity? In that environment how would you be different? In that environment would you love yourself enough to be more, give more, and have fun doing so?

Let me help you imagine it. By adding the essence of love to the work environment you would feel safe and secure. Going to work would give you pleasure and an unprecedented willingness to be vulnerable and trusting. Your fear of loss would decrease or be eliminated, and you would know you were cared for, seen, and known. It would be an environment where you gave your very best to yourself and to your company. It would be "home."

Love is The Strategic Advantage™. It can change everything about your work environment: the morale, innovation, willingness to change, and consequently, it can change the bottom-line.

Love in the 21st century workplace is a foundational piece of change management. It is how you and your company will differentiate and position yourselves both inwardly and outwardly. From the outwardly facing perspective, you've got love as the foundational piece of marketing and customer experience, i.e. this is what you do, and you love it, you love your customers, and this is fundamental to how you operate your business. This is a well-worn path in terms of marketing and a company's outward message, but very few truly execute love as their strategic advantage.

What about the inwardly facing position? How do you operate from a position of love? How do you build on the actions of giving, responding, respecting, knowing, having the humility to be intimate with your work, committing and caring in how and who you hire? Is it in every nook and cranny of your operational systems? Is it part of crafting your efficiency? During the cry for urgency, do you still hold to the tenets of love as a strategic advantage? Are the actions of love in every aspect of the creating, recreating, and running your business? If not, you will fail in the 21st century workplace. The old ways do not work!

You may say, "This is not so different than what my work place is trying to create now." If so, congratulations. But what is lost in even the most ambitious reformers of 21st century business is the foundational emotion that we're going for in customer centricity, in trying to find a balance (work/life), in corporate responsibility—it's love in all its practical, and executable aspects.

Many CEO's know change is being demanded of them. In fact, 92 percent of CEOs of privately owned companies said, according to the "19th Annual Global CEO Survey (2016), "that they will have to change how they manage their brand, marketing, and communications." What this report does not say is that they don't know how to do that. Another article from Price Waterhouse Cooper calls them "undaunted but underprepared." [1]

They are not alone; the world is underprepared. We know not only that the world is crumbling, but that the solutions to business issues that worked in the past no longer work. CEOs are scrambling to discover what else will work. Love is their strategic advantage, if they can harness and understand its power.

It's time for the wisdom-leaders to step up. Once, we held in the highest esteem the knowledge workers, i.e., the well-trained, technologically-astute professionals. Now it is past time for the wisdom-worker, and the wisdom-leaders to take their stand as the midwives of the new way of business in the 21st century. This term, wisdom-leaders was taught to me by Robert Rose, one of the premier content managers in consulting today. When we kicked around the idea of CEOs who have moved beyond emotional intelligence (EQ) to wisdom-leader, we couldn't find any obvious examples. That doesn't mean they are not out there birthing their piece of the new world. It just means that they are not yet as visible as we need them to be.

So, what is a wisdom-leader?

- They have mastered and moved beyond knowledge and skill, and integrated their strengths and powers.

- Such leaders are delighted with the "fool," i.e., the one willing to appropriately risk and jump into the unknown with both feet, but they do not tolerate the foolish.

- They are willing to embrace new concepts such as "love as the strategic advantage."

- They grow impatient with those who are enamored with themselves.

- They celebrate before, during, and after any major project. They hold gratitude as one of the highest tenets of life. They understand that celebration and gratitude beget the same.

- They rejoice in your triumphs, but do not countenance the arrogant.

- They listen to the voices of those who have stepped into their own power and give no attention to the self-serving.

- They seek out and encourage those with wise judgment and do not tolerate the judgmental.

- They laugh with joy in the presence of your mastery and artistry and mourn when you do not reach for them.

- Crucially, these leaders, who know we are in a time of the unknown, do not expect themselves to have all the answers. Rather they co-create answers with others.

The true wisdom-leader knows that for everyone in the workplace to give their best, those same people must know that what they do matters, and that they can and do make a difference. Humans are wired to seek meaning in everything they do, and the wisdom leader encourages that seeking.

Clearly, the qualities of love described earlier are needed in the new world, and most certainly in businesses that will flourish in the 21st century. Times have changed, people have changed; the most talented have shifted their goals and desires, customers have become savvier. The world is a different place and will continue to change at an unprecedented speed.

Where better to learn about what you have a right to expect from the place where you spend most of your waking hours than in a book about love? Love is the strategic advantage. Its time has come. To quote one of my favorite bards, singer John Legend, "We're the generation. We can't afford to wait. The future started yesterday and we're already late."

I know it is not too late!

Kimberley Heart

[1] "Undaunted, but underprepared? A private company view from the 20th CEO Survey." PWC 20th CEO Survey. Accessed November 4, 2017.

Natural Balance

"Happiness is not a matter of intensity,
but of balance and order and rhythm and harmony."
~ Thomas Merton

C aring for yourself will increase your capacity to care for others. You know this already. Where are you in balance? On a daily basis?

I have been using this self-care scale for years. I have been practicing some sort of self-care, seeking balance, my entire adult life. This was a natural response to compassion fatigue (Figley, 1995)[2], or burnout. It was a natural response to an overactive nervous system: prone to anxiety, with a quick stress response. I was intensely inquisitive, analytical, and passionate about life. At 19, I had a moment of clarity, divine inspiration really, and I know that I had no choice but to be of service. I enthusiastically entered a profession where I could support individuals going through severe trauma, addiction, child custody problems, and legal issues. I thought my passion would buffer me from the emotional toll, but soon came to realize that it would not!

In my line of work, our longevity in the field depends on creating balance, natural rhythms. It is very easy to become depleted from caring too much when it is out of balance. It ripples out and affects overall quality of life, including work and family life, and overall health and well-being.

I was 24 when I completed graduate school, and started my first professional job. This was during the mid-90's at the height of the AIDS epidemic. Women were, unknowingly, the fastest growing sector of the HIV population. Infection was typically contracted because of an abusive relationship and/or related drug abuse. I was in a position to supervise a small team of outreach workers who walked around town offering support in high-risk communities. The team was made up of counselors who had lived through experiences, including domestic violence, childhood trauma and abuse, addiction and mental health issues. I learned as much from them as I had in grad school.

I never imagined such violence was possible in one person's history. During this time, I worked with an amazing woman (my supervisor at the time) who eventually became a mentor and friend. I learned that she was one of the founding leaders of the domestic violence movement. The work was cutting edge, and eventually we started a unique set of domestic abuse programs for women with addiction and mental health issues – services not offered together anywhere in the county.

Love Revolution

In the early years I actually left the agency to travel and worked for a nongovernmental organization (NGO) in Palestine. I was away for about 2 years. This was a re-balancing experience. My need for balance always involved physicality mixed with some novelty. I immediately took up hiking in the local mountains as a natural counterpart to working in an office and on the gritty urban streets. That workout turned into mountain biking and bike touring. During my time away, I traveled by bike through Europe, then trekked the Annapurna trail in Nepal on the way back home.

After returning and settling back into my life, I discovered I had a newfound commitment to the essence of work in the U.S. – social change. The intensity of it all brought on a deep need for balance and re-balancing: balance changed from time to time based on my age and life situation/experience at the moment. I got in touch with my spirituality. When I returned, I got into Kundalini yoga which offered exercises, meditation, and metaphysics.

I learned to ski (great fun!) and worked as a children's therapist at a mental health clinic for a short while. I returned to my old agency to start up the Domestic Violence programs, and also began to date the man who would become my husband.

When my son was born, I worked part time for a few years. My son was a high need kid, with ADHD, Tourette's and OCD.

I learned how to train other service providers on issues and interventions which eventually led to my hire as an adjunct professor at the University of Southern California (USC). Many non-profits are dysfunctional, and this agency was no exception. It got so messy that the founder left and hired a replacement who had a different, more conventional vision for the agency.

My balancing needs shifted, and I began a meditation routine that continues to evolve organically: from 15 minutes of yoga breathing to nearly 2 hours of sitting and movement based open focus meditation. After 14 years, I left that agency to teach as an adjunct professor at USC, and also started a private therapy practice. It was all very stressful. I maintained a workout routine because I noticed my mood and mental clarity benefited from it. I became creative at scheduling this self-care time.

I have used natural balancing techniques with clients suffering from a range of trauma-intensive (often trauma-based) symptoms, as well as employees (counselors, therapists, managers) in trauma-based social service programs. I have used them for training purposes and for graduate students. In all cases, individuals found that they were neglecting certain areas of life. It also brought attention to the areas that they were caring for adequately.

It is no accident that the "giving" field is primarily made up of women. We are naturally the caregivers and the nurturers. This is reinforced in our society. This is a gift. However, when it is out of balance – life goes awry. Balance requires receiving without a negative charge attached, as well as self-care (or self-giving) with compassion. When in balance, we thrive. In my field, we sometimes call this "compassion satisfaction."

In order to be in balance, we have to care for all areas – mind, body, and spirit – which includes the emotional/psychological, intellectual, relational, and physical. If one area is neglected, we are out of balance, sometimes with great consequences. Balance can be easy. It simply requires your attention and commitment.

Having worked with women, I am painfully aware of the guilt that ensues in nurturing oneself, and practicing self-care. Often, I am met with feelings of inadequacy, self-doubt and of being undeserving. It actually helps to nurture oneself with the thought of being more available to others.

Today, I incorporate self-care into my life and into my therapy practice. It is an ongoing effort to keep in balance. Research on yoga and the brain is astounding! If a yoga posture with a mantra or affirmation is practiced throughout the day, 6 to 8 times, for as little as 30 seconds, our brain becomes more integrated and balanced over time. Practicing six or more times throughout the day can work wonders. This practice should include the same move and affirmation for 6 weeks in order to see results. Research is a result of the explosion of the combination of neuroscience and trauma (van der Kolk, 2014; Diyankova, 2017; Villemure e al., 2015). I invite you to test it out and give it a try.

Take the self-care test. This test is short and to the point. It will naturally highlight areas that have been neglected. For example, when I am working with a group of people, I sometimes find that folks are doing a decent job of eating healthy and spending time with family and hitting the gym. However, one area may be out of alignment.

For example, Ginny was a caseworker at a local drug and alcohol center. She ate a healthy diet and worked out regularly. This came easy. However, when she completed her self-assessment, she noticed that her spiritual practice had been neglected. Ginny's drive to "give back" was based on a spiritual sense of giving to a greater cause and, in fact, was based on her spiritual belief system. Her practice was that of giving thanks, sitting in reflection and contemplation and spending time in nature. She realized that she had let this practice go when she entered graduate school to advance her training in psychotherapy. She also became aware that she was feeling depleted and run down.

Check out the following Self Care Assessment:

> https://mnliteracy.org/sites/default/files/self-care_assesment.pdf

And this site contains the Self-Assessment Tool:

> http://aceresponse.org/img/uploads/file/self_care_que
> stionnaire.pdf

Now take a few moments to consider the following questions:

- How do you find balance?

- What keeps you from being in balance?

- How do you check in with yourself?

- How do you re-balance when falling out of alignment? (this always happens)

This is a quick guide (for busy people) with morning, noon and night calming, centering rituals.

1. MORNING

What is your morning routine? Do you crawl out of bed, drag yourself through your morning duties, and finally wake up after your 3rd cup of coffee at the office? Time is precious, especially for busy parents. We work hard to give our children the best opportunities in life but sometimes we just miss out on our own. Morning is the prime time for setting your day. Every sunrise is an opportunity for rebirth, recreation. Most parents I work with, and that I know, are running out the door, rushing their children to get to school on time. Oftentimes there is frustration and even yelling/arguing. Can you give yourself 5 extra minutes in the morning to create a more harmonious entry into the day?

My commitment is:

_____

_____

_____

_____

HOW MUCH TIME DO YOU HAVE?

My journey started (sort of) when I decided to take an intro to Kundalini Yoga at a local center as a birthday gift to myself – I had just turned 30. The teachings and classes were wonderful. I still practice it today. It is truly an ancient mind-body-spirit practice. One day, the yoga instructor offered to give students specific meditations to try at home. Of course, I thought I was too busy but he convinced me otherwise. His perspective was, "Aren't you worth 5 minutes a day?"

So, I took home the CD with a 5 minute chant (guru, Wahe guru) which was designed to induce peace. It was recorded with beautiful, peaceful music. The discipline of Kundalini suggests that you practice the same chant every day for 40 days for tangible, lasting results. This formula has also been demonstrated by neuroscience studies.

If you have 5 minutes:

- Get up a few minutes early.

- Gaze at the light – whether it's an emerging dawn or the rays of the sunrise or patchy clouds. I generally rise while it's dark and look for the morning moon. Sometimes it's shimmering on the ocean and truly spectacular.

- Sit with your spine erect for five minutes listening to a meditation or music that you enjoy, to feel grounded and peaceful.

- Set an intention for your day.

- Go outside or sit by a window and listen to birds chirping. Birds have a natural rhythm and tend to begin morning chirps around dawn. Aligning with this for a few minutes will provide more balance.

If you have 15 minutes:

Awesome! This segment will feel so good!

- Spend five minutes stretching. I have a Kundalini Yoga routine that I have been using for years. I also use a 5-minute routine from Donna Eden's energy medicine to get the body moving, blood moving, and vibration humming. This movement helps my body to wake up and sets my mind for some mindfulness practice.

- Headspace (https://headspace.com/) – free app for mindfulness for beginners – my clients love this and it is particularly useful for the left-brained type.

- Hay House – more spiritually based – has lots and lots of free meditations and visitations. Give it a try!

If you have 25 minutes:

- Stretch and sit in meditation for 15 minutes – this is awesome.

- Turn your morning routine into a giving and receiving ritual. Be in the moment. Count your breaths. Bless the abundant food that you are preparing for your family.

My commitment is:

_____

_____

_____

_____

2. AFTERNOON

Have a healthy lunch, take a break, and lunch with some friends.

- Now that I work for myself, I don't have a lunchroom to go chat with co-workers. It was always fun to connect at this time. Sometimes I work from my home office as does my husband. Occasionally, we have the chance to lunch together and I will typically stop what I'm doing and enjoy.

3. EVENING

- Pleasure reading.

- Bathe with bath salts – I do both every evening.

Regularly schedule exercise. The key is to enjoy it.

I love the benefits and the process. I have days where I go to the gym and take sculpting classes – light weight classes. The benefits are quick and lasting.

Other days, I hit the local trails for a 45-minute hike: listening to a meditation as I walk., or just observing the natural surroundings – ocean, trees, and birds.

My commitment is

_____

_____

_____

_____

Balance

Rejuvenate

Reflect

Debbie Murad

[2] Figley, C.R. 1995. "Compassion fatigue as secondary traumatic stress disorder: An overview." In Compassion fatigue: Coping with secondary traumatic stress disorder in those who treat the traumatized, Edited by: Figley, C.R. 1–20. New York: Brunner/Mazel.

The Power of Permission

"Perfect love casts out fear"
~ 1 John 4:18

My most honest moments have occurred in front of the mirror. For a long time, I preferred not to look, but on one particular day, I did. What I saw wasn't pretty – a listless (almost lifeless) woman with no light in her eyes.

I was trying to convince myself that my life was enough. After all, I had chosen it, hadn't I? This marriage? I had said "yes" all those years before.

But of course, none of us knows where one decision will lead. I had not imagined mine would ever lead here to this place of desolation in the midst of marriage, motherhood and ministry in the church my husband and I had served in for the previous ten years.

It was my birthday. I was turning forty. I looked in the mirror for telltale wrinkles on my face and couldn't find them. I still looked young. I should have been happy. I was doing well for forty and I still had half my life ahead of me.

Tears welled in my eyes and through them I imagined the age lines etching into my fine skin, the muscles beginning to sag, the way computer simulations predict aging. I knew one thing: I couldn't live like this for another 40 years. How could I live like this for one more day? If I was turning eighty now, there would be the comfort of knowing it was almost over.

I reeled from shock at my own thoughts. Here I stood at forty and my one birthday wish, in the solitude of my own heart, was to be turning eighty. Because then maybe I could die.

The moment of honesty that comes in the depth of darkness shines the light that can set us free. It strips away all the pretense, all the coping mechanisms we have put in place to get through each day, all our best intentions, and the brave face we wear as we do what is right and what is expected of us. All the strategies that keep us functioning hide from us the grim reality beneath: that our souls are slowly dying from lack of air and a lack of love.

Love. That was missing from my marriage, yes. But I was about to go on a journey that would reveal how it was also missing from within me. I had no idea how to love myself. If you'd asked me then I would have dismissed the idea as self-indulgent and selfish. I had sought to love other people so faithfully for so long, both in my family and in my church, that I had all but disappeared. I had mistaken duty for love, sacrifice for commitment. And I had lost all sense of myself.

In that moment of honesty, the shock of my utter hopelessness – the desire to die – woke me. It tripped a wire somewhere in my brain. It yelled that something was wrong and finally I heard it. My survival instinct kicked in. I knew I had to do something. I had to save myself.

Divorce was the answer I didn't want to face. My church-taught beliefs meant that door was closed. I had promised "Till death do us part," and promises were not to be broken. I realized with absolute clarity that this was the reason I wanted to die: death was the only way out.

All I can say is that my soul objected. It objected in groans with the deepest truth in all the universe – Love.

I knew this truth. God is Love. I am loved. This was the underlying principle of everything I believed, yet somehow my imperfect adherence to faithfulness had led me to this place where the only way out was death. Something had gone wrong. How did things ever get this twisted?

I had to radically rethink my life. There had to be a different way to look at this. The principle of love could not lead to such desolation.

So, I gave myself permission to think about my life and what I believed differently.

PERMISSION

Shifting my world view required time, commitment, research and a deep trust that it was okay to even just explore the alternatives. I could do none of this until I gave myself permission.

Whenever we want to change something in our lives, we must start with this principle of giving ourselves permission. For unless we acknowledge our freedom to explore, and grant ourselves the opportunity, we will never take the first step to change anything in our lives, big or small. Ordinarily, we give ourselves permission subconsciously, before we embark on anything new. But when the change we face is scary, potentially threatening, or likely to meet with the disapproval of others (as divorce was for me), we might need to consciously authorize ourselves just to look at the possibility.

This sort of deep belief-shifting work is not easy. It must be accompanied by a commitment to self-care. As I've already mentioned, I had lost any tangible sense of who I was beneath the duties and cares of my life. As I began to explore change, I instinctively knew I had to take care of myself. I had to reconnect with my soul, so my true values could guide me on my journey, keeping me nourished and safe. I found a simple way to strengthen my heart.

I looked back to happier times in my life to find something that had brought me joy, to see if I could rekindle a little of that feeling. Was there something I once found pleasure in doing, that I could do again to sustain me on this journey?

I remembered in my younger days that I had written poetry. I loved carefully selecting the words I needed to express my soul, stringing them together in rhythms that sang life to me. I was sure, if I tried, I could do this again. And so, I did.

Is there something that sang to you many years ago that you thought you outgrew or that was crowded out by other grown-up responsibilities? Or simply something that got lost in the passage of time? For you it may be painting, dancing, gardening, swimming, singing karaoke style while you're doing the ironing (that one was a life-saver for me too!).

Or it could be something you always dreamt of doing, but never did. For example, taking singing or horseback riding lessons. If so, this is your chance. Take it. Do something for yourself, just because it makes you happy.

Whatever else may be going on in your life, these pockets of me-time can be treasured as moments of pure joy: avenues of relief that can sustain you along the way.

Doing this simple thing for yourself is deep self-care. In doing this thing you love, you show yourself you are worthy – worthy to enjoy life and be happy. You start to reconnect with who you are as you express yourself through this simple activity. It may be through creative expression as it was for me: writing poetry, putting thoughts to paper and learning to know myself again. Or the self-expression could come equally through other means, including the exhilaration of physical activity that breathes life back into your body and soul.

Honor yourself with this gift of love.

As I examined my beliefs surrounding divorce and looked to the wisdom of others, I knew this was a spiritual journey and that it was my faith I was scrutinizing. I found others who professed faith in God, who also believed divorce was possible within the bounds of that faith. On the surface, this was what I needed. But of course, I also needed to ground this new belief into my soul. I needed to own it for myself, to trust in its goodness and its truth. I needed to align it with that core value of the universe: Love.

If I couldn't do that, I was as stuck as ever. I felt the fear rising. When I thought of getting this wrong, of falling out of divine favor, the fear swirled in my stomach. My whole body would tense and tremor. I wanted my marriage to end, but what if God turned his back on me? What if I lost my faith?

The terror these thoughts held for me was immense. Yet as soon as they rose I was able to calm them and send them gently on their way. They returned, but each time I sent them gently away, knowing they held no power over me.

I could do this only because I trusted in that deep truth of Love. It is true that Love conquers fear. Fear cannot stand in its presence. Despite all the turmoil and uncertainty that surrounded me, I knew without a shadow of a doubt that I stood in the presence of divine Love and being there, whatever choice I ultimately made, I could not fall from grace.

Do you have that firm foundational belief where you know you are spiritually supported by love? When you trust in what your soul knows, you can withstand any part of your earthly journey because you know that ultimately you are secure.

I recommend a visualization technique to support you in this deep knowing. Whenever fear or doubt creeps in, when you face conflict in your spirit or conflict with others, you can use this visualization to access the peace of divine presence.

For this practice, close your eyes and take some deep, calming breaths. Take as many as you need until you are transported to a place of peace in your mind's eye. My place is a beach at night. When I visualize this beach, I see the moon shining on the dark sea. I feel the water lapping around my bare ankles. I hear nothing but the waves gently hitting the shoreline. I smell the salt air and taste it on my tongue. I luxuriate under the stars. I let the feeling of calm wash over me, then enter my spirit. This is where I know divine presence. This is where I know I am safe.

The first time you do this, you'll discover the place of peace and presence that is your sanctuary. Is it a forest glade, or on the dizzy heights of a mountain top? In a childhood den? By a cool river? Don't be tempted to anticipate where it will be. Trust that you will find your way there as you breathe in and out. When you are there, take your time,. Explore it with all five of your senses as I did, so it becomes clear and familiar to you. And feel the divine presence of Spirit supporting you in Love.

Once you know this place and how it feels, you will learn to close your eyes and return there. Sometimes you'll only have an instant, but that will be long enough to know you are divinely supported and to have your heart strengthened in this knowledge. You will know then that whatever stress or challenge you are facing, you will survive and you will overcome. As I did.

This is faith.

Love Revolution

In leaving my marriage, I learned that rather than losing my faith as I had been led to fear, I strengthened it. I trusted in a new path. Not knowing what life would look like next, not knowing who would stand with me and who would be against me, but knowing that divine presence – God who is Love – would not leave me.

Love casts out Fear.

Trust yourself enough to know the Love that supports you and resides within you. Give yourself the permission you need for your journey. Love yourself with the simple gift of a little me-time along the way. Know the safety of your inner place of divine presence. And step into your transformation.

Christina Sharp

How To Love Yourself
Out of Darkness

"The most beautiful people we have known are those who have known defeat, known suffering, known struggle, known loss, and have found their way out of those depths."
~ Elisabeth Kübler-Ross

I'm sitting in my office looking out my window. It's Ireland, so as usual, the sky is dreary and covered in a thick layer of grey cloud. The day is menacing us with lashing rain and icy winds, and there's a certain dullness in the color of the sky that begs for a good book and a roaring fire.

I think back to where I was 4 years ago. Moving to Ireland against my wishes, all I could see were the storms and hurricanes experienced on a daily basis. It was like a climatic representation of what lived inside me. Ireland is a long way from my previous home in Spain where the sun shone 350 days a year. But then again, I'm a long way from that previous version of me. I was the person who half-laughed and fake-smiled through life, hiding away the fear and sorrow that lived inside. Hiding away the "knowing" that I wasn't really good enough to be loved or that I deserved anything truly good. The person who believed that if I just tried a little harder, smiled a little longer, helped a little more and never shed a tear – that everyone would like me better and that maybe, finally, at some point, everything I'd ever wanted would come my way.

But that's not how life works.

You don't get what you deserve simply because you try. You deserve only what you're committed to. And you're only ever truly committed to what you love.

There are all sorts of notions around love. Society teaches us that love is putting someone else's needs before our own. Duty and marriage often lead us to think that love means sacrifice and compromise. For me, love meant putting my life and dreams on the back burner in order to give my husband what he needed and wanted, for his career and happiness. Then, when the kids came along, love meant adding them to the priority list ahead of myself.

I did this willingly.

I loved them – I love them – with all my heart, soul and existence. And despite being last on my priority list, I still managed to achieve 3 diplomas, an executive position, my own catering company and was the host of my own TV show…all in all, on a résumé, I wasn't doing too bad.

But life is more than accomplishments. Happiness is made up of the moments that lie between. Love comes from a place that lets us know that all is good. Love provides security, reassurance and certainty. And on that night – that night when I sat eagerly waiting for my husband to come home, butterflies in my stomach, excited to see him after his business trip and to start our Christmas holidays together – I was taken aback when an unexpected conversation thread popped up on our iPad. He was making plans to meet another woman.

When I called him with love and a certain level of naiveté and disbelief, his uncharacteristic response crushed me. "Stop fucking nagging me! My phone is dying and I need it for emergencies," he said. "The only emergencies would be work or family. You are with your team and I am your family. Who else are you expecting?" I sheepishly replied. He just hung up. At that moment, everything changed. All the security I had in our future together disappeared. All the reassurance in things being well, vanished. All the certainty that I was loved was obliterated.

I had given so much to my husband's happiness that I had forgotten my own. I'd been so busy loving my husband more than I loved myself that I forgot to be committed to me. To love me! To take care of me! And to make me happy. I forgot to treat myself with the same love and respect I gave others. Starting over at 40, in a new country, with no local friends to lean on for support, with a baby and 2 small daughters who needed me 24/7, with no job to fall back on, and no savings to leave Ireland as I wanted to… I cried like I'd never cried before. I cried with shame and judgment. I cried with fear and anger. I cried for all that I ever wanted and never got. I cried for broken dreams and lost opportunities. I cried with hatred. I cried for me.

I felt guilty when he blamed me for his cheating. I felt abandoned and rejected by love. I felt deceived by life. I didn't know what to believe anymore. I became unable to trust the words and actions of everyone around me. I judged myself with pain for everything I'd ever experienced: I was unworthy; I was unlovable; I was too strong; I was too weak.

I didn't sleep for 13 days. I didn't eat or drink for 13 days. I didn't speak to a soul for 13 days. I just cried. My thoughts circled maniacally in my head, for 13 days, until the tears dried out and there was nothing left in me to shed. I was empty… Until something in me shifted.

It was like a bolt of lightning hit me in the heart.

I realized, in that instant, that perhaps I had created the situation that allowed him to seek whatever made him happy, regardless of what it cost me. After all, I'd given up everything I'd built (friends, business and my career on TV) to start over in Ireland for his career and happiness. Was this love? If so, the love for whom? Certainly not myself. You would never ask someone you love to give up so much even if that someone is you.

Love Revolution

I realized that this is what I'd been taught all my life. To give. To sacrifice. To put others before me. I was good at it. Scratch that. I was great at it! Loving someone else was easier than loving myself. Putting others first meant having an excuse and someone else to blame when I didn't get what I wanted – when I wasn't happy.

In an instant, I stopped crying, got out of bed and into the shower, as if to cleanse the old me away. I stopped seeing all the pain and injustice. I stopped seeing the tragedy and insult. I stopped seeing what had been done to me and started seeing how everything had happened for me. This was my opportunity. This was my time. That dark period didn't break me – it made me stronger, wiser, able to understand what I wanted from life. What I truly wanted from life. It made me more determined. It gave me clarity over my values and set the boundaries for what I would no longer accept.

I suddenly understood what truly mattered to me. I realized my purpose. I realized how much I'd always loved everyone unconditionally, except myself. I realized that everything I'd ever said or done that was tinged with embarrassment, fear, anger, sadness, resentment or jealousy, was a cry from my soul to pay attention to what I needed to love myself. I realized that even the difficulty I had accepting a compliment graciously, with a simple thank you, was showing me an area where I could grow to love myself more. And, now, I could clearly put myself at the top of that priority list because I knew how important it was to do so.

To see the light, you have to crack the darkness. And that means being willing to go into the darkness within. To accept the mistakes made and the decisions taken. To take hold of the pain and say, "I own you!" so that you can begin to see it through new eyes. So that you can take responsibility for who you are, what you have and how much love you get.

And to do so, the first step is to:

FORGET EVERYTHING YOU'VE EVER BEEN TAUGHT ABOUT LOVE

This is not an easy thing to do. After all, everything we do and say is a reflection of who we are – our identity. We spend our lives proving who we are to the world by the actions we take and the words we use, hoping that these are enough for the acceptance of others and that they will take us to where we want to go in our dreams. Most of us give because we want the world to see us as givers, as kind and generously loving human beings. We expect that by being givers, others will give back, thus proving our worth, and appreciation in their eyes.

But you are not reading this to continue on the same journey you've been on all of these years. Because if you have ever felt anger, sadness or hurt, there is a distinct possibility that everything you've ever been taught about love is wrong.

I'm not saying you have to stop giving. I'm saying you have to give in a different way. With a different motivation. With a different standard, and without expectations from others.

Life is a journey of self-awareness – of conscious living – and unimaginable love-making. And the first person you need to make love to is yourself – through and through – inside and out – with fabulous lavishness and unapologetic gratuity – 24/7 – 365 & $\frac{1}{4}$ days a year. And I'm going to show you how.

HOW I MAKE LOVE TO MYSELF

When you're re-examining your life, the first thing you tend to do is judge yourself. Judging is rarely if ever, an act of love. I had to learn how not to judge before I could move on with my healing and create a life filled with unimaginable love-making to myself. There is love and there is unconditional love. To truly love yourself (and others), the latter is key.

So, what is "Unconditional Love"?

Unconditional love has become one of those terms we so easily mention in conversation. We all talk about how we want it in our lives, our relationships, our friendships. We each believe that we are big givers of it in our lives, our relationships and our friendships. We throw this term around like the latest craze that decides your level of coolness or apathy for society's current trends. But Unconditional

Love, true unconditional love, is actually a very hard thing to find and it's no wonder why.

The most powerful example in our understanding of unconditional love is the unconditional love of God. Whatever your religious beliefs, God's love is taught to us in schools, at home, in church and in our culture. Have you ever noticed the mixed message of God's unconditional love? God's love is filled with conditions. We learn, from a very young age, that there are some very strict rules to obey if you want to be granted a spot in Heaven. And a lot of less admirable (and some would argue, more natural) actions, thoughts and behaviors that will lead you into Hell. When we are led by fear, is there any real hope for love?

And what about our society's take on unconditional love? What if antiquated psychological theories have us searching for labels that lead us to believe that we're broken instead of whole? What if we are all being conditioned to explain our thoughts and actions as an example of our lack of self-worth, lack of self-love, lack of self-appreciation? Is judging ourselves and believing that we are "not enough" acceptable thinking for an intelligent and reasonable human being nowadays? Is society teaching us to love unconditionally when it inherently believes certain emotions are unacceptable and must be treated?

"Unconditional" means "without conditions", otherwise described as: without rules, expectations, reasons, excuses or conditions of any kind.

And "love"? Well, that one is a little tougher to explain. When I researched the term "Love" many different definitions came up. So I'd like to offer my own. To me, love is complete understanding. Where there is judgment, there is no understanding.

LOVE IS APPRECIATION WITHOUT ANY JUDGMENT

What would happen if with everyone you met, you loved with complete understanding (without judgment, rules, expectations or conditions)? What if you loved yourself that way?

Imagine it for a second.

No action would ever make you angry.

No word would leave you unhappy.

Nothing that ever went on around you or within you would ever disturb your inner peace.

Because with unconditional love, you could see that every time you were triggered by someone's words or actions (even yours), it wasn't against you, it was for you! It was a gift, an opportunity to understand, to learn, to grow, to assume your rightful place on this planet as the super-duper-human-vessel-for-all-things-eternal that you are. Your life, your parenting, your friendships, your relationships, your employment, your leadership, your entire legacy could be graced with love and understanding.

With more unconditional love, there would be less room for doubt, fear, regret, anger, and sadness. There would be less questioning of your self-worth, self-love, or level of self-appreciation. All actions and words would be understood as the purest form of shining who you are to the world, your identity in all its glory, without censoring. Your existence would be pure, abundant and joyful. Your accomplishments would be unlimited, extraordinary, and unstoppable.

There would be no more need for acceptance or forgiveness because both of these imply that at some point, even if only for a moment, there was a judgment.

Everything would be perfect as it is because nothing would have any meaning other than being perfect.

We would live in peace.

You would live in peace.

What would your life look like with unconditional self-love? With the confidence to shine the real you and your identity, your standards and values? What if you allowed yourself to experience absolute inner peace?

Love Revolution

This is what I had to do for myself. To understand what was truly important to me. To know where my boundaries of acceptable behavior rested. To become intimate with who I am and who I want to be. To commit to loving myself unconditionally with absolute determination. To stop judging. To appreciate myself for who I was.

To simply:

L – Let it flow

O – Observe what pops up

V – Value my truth

E – Elevate my personal standards

A funny thing happens when you start to let go of the anger, hurt and pain you've suffered. You grow freedom. And freedom is just another way of saying that you get to do what you want on your own terms. Where disapproving opinions no longer matter. Where judgment no longer lives.

Turning judgment into love is simple, but it does take a little time to get used to it, and the awareness and willingness to make the change in yourself.

L O V E

I LOVE every day of my life, especially whenever I find myself "disrupted" by a word or action. I teach my clients to LOVE so that they can learn to appreciate themselves more, in a very short time. To LOVE is to set yourself free from the burden and weight of negatively judging yourself and others.

L – LET IT FLOW

After my long shower that day, I wrote down everything I felt, everything I was angry, sad and disappointed with. It was a long exercise. I had so much to get off my chest. So much regret and unhappiness laid on my shoulders, which had been stiff with pain for well over 10 years. By the time I was done, I had over 20 pages written out.

When you do this exercise, I invite you to be colorful in your language. To be petty. To be nasty. To throw in as many F-bombs as you wish (it's OK. Science has proven that it's good for you!).

In order to let it go, you've got to let it flow. So let every emotion flow through you in your writing.

O – OBSERVE WHAT POPS UP

Once you've finished getting everything out of your head and off your chest and you have it down on paper, go back to the beginning and start reading through your notes. Observe all of the expectations that popped up. Highlight or underline any place where you believed the outcome should've been different from what actually happened;

where your expectation did not meet the reality. Hint: the word "should" in any statement is a good indication of an unmet expectation.

V – VALUE YOUR TRUTH

Each expectation that was unmet lets you know what is important to you. It shows you what your beliefs and rules of life are. It tells you who you are.

This is where the true you lives. This is you! Honor it. Appreciate it. Love it! You are perfect just as you are. You are a gift. You don't get unsettled because something is wrong. You get unsettled because reality clashes with your identity, your expectations, your standards. Your standards represent what is important to you.

E – ELEVATE YOUR PERSONAL STANDARDS

From now on, you know exactly how to raise your standards and the quality of your life because now you know how to recognize them. Any time you feel unsettled, you'll know you're being shown exactly what you need to know to make you happy. You can decide to live according to what matters to you. To make decisions based on your values. To live in harmony with the real you.

In short, whenever something triggers a response in you, rather than judge it, look at it! Find the expectation that reality didn't represent and the standard that wasn't met, and learn something new about yourself. See it without judgment. Appreciate that others may not have the same expectations or values as you, and that's ok. They are living according to who they are. Remember, you can't change them any more than they can change you.

Your anger, your sadness, your guilt, your regret... They are gifts! They are messages! They're telling you where to find your freedom and happiness. They are showing you how to make unimaginable love to yourself by Loving yourself Unconditionally.

L.O.V.E – Let it flow. Observe it. Value your truth. Elevate your standards

It's all a part of the miraculous, beautiful, and unique you.

A lot has happened since those 13 days of tears. Ireland still has the same grey skies... but now it provides a softening, calming energy to life's hustle. Those grey skies bring perspective and introspection, inner knowledge and peace, understanding and unconditional love to everything that I do.

My husband and I decided to go our separate ways. Sometimes strangers become best friends and then go back to being strangers again. It's not what I expected from life, but our good time together and my three magnificent daughters are some of the gifts that marriage gave me. In the end, we realized that we did not share the same beliefs about marriage and family. It was a painful lesson when it happened, but a lesson that has allowed me to learn who I truly am and how to unconditionally love myself. I no longer sacrifice and compromise what's important to me. Thoroughly enjoying my life, being a positive role model for my daughters and for anyone who meets me, is something I value strongly. This has led me to achieve a lot of wonderful things that don't fit on a résumé.

After I stopped crying, I joined a gym and went from having a mom body to a body I am proud of. I went to Los Angeles and created a huge network of professional support and growth that I am thankful for (it has become my second, and sunnier, home). I published my first book, and completely re-invented my life to serve and help as many people as I can live with more love, happiness and fulfillment. My daughters and I are tighter than ever thanks to a deeper understanding of who they are. (Through my work on LOVE, I've learnt to nurture their individuality instead of raising them according to my expectations of them.) I love every moment of this journey because I have more awareness of living by what I value. I live fully. I travel, I meet fascinating people who share the same love for others as I do. My relationships are stronger and more fulfilling than ever before. I laugh from deep inside my belly and I smile because I am happy. My shoulders never hurt again.

I do work that means something to me, to my soul, and to my legacy on this earth. I rarely feel fear, doubt or self-judgment. I can say "thank you" at a compliment and take it on board without questioning it. Living by what's important to me means that there's an inner knowing that I deserve the very best because I am worthy and committed to having it. I'm more confident, more loving and understanding of everyone around me. I am more patient and peaceful. I'm grateful in my core for all that I am and for all that has happened with my ex-husband – after all, without it, I would not have experienced a crack in my darkness for the light of unconditional love to shine in.

And once you've experienced Unconditional Love, true unconditional love, there will never be any darkness again.

Carla M. Jones

Learning to Love Yourself

"Learning to Love Yourself, Is The Greatest Love of All"
~ Linda Creed

My godmother, Linda Creed, has been my inspiration throughout my life and I always come back to the words in her song, "The Greatest Love of All." She found self-love while she was suffering with breast cancer. After watching Linda's self-love journey through cancer, I realized that part of my path was to learn to love myself unconditionally and to then love others unconditionally as well.

Shortly after college, my parents divorced, and I decided to move to Chicago. Little did I know that this s where my personal journey would begin. When I arrived, I met a woman who could help me navigate my new surroundings. The first words out of her mouth were, "This was no accident." I later learned that "there are no accidents." It was not surprising that she is a healer. She is a certified Reiki Master/Teacher, and a licensed clinical psychotherapist.

I immediately pursued Reiki One in the Usui Reiki Ryoho Lineage, became certified in Reiki Two, and then became a Certified Reiki Master/Teacher. This was a fabulous fit for me, not only because I was doing what I loved and chose with my heart, but this was a big leap further into my self-love journey. This started me on my path to following my life's destiny and to learn my true purpose.

During these past twenty years, I dove into everything that felt right on my journey including: my individual truth, energy work, following self-guidance, raising my vibration, learning and teaching heart versus ego, releasing karmic cycles, forgiveness, meditation, higher consciousness and, in turn, finding self-love and actualization. I believe in awakening. Following these steps will be the most important and rewarding accomplishments you could ever achieve in this lifetime. These are some of the key points to attaining the life of your dreams.

HIGHER PURPOSE

We are all here in this life for a reason. We are here to awaken to our full potential, create the life of our dreams and to bring those dreams into reality. You came here to create "your" reality/life, not "have it happen to you." Change your perception and realize now that your life is responding to you and your thoughts. Therefore, it's a prerequisite to create and dream up that life in your head and heart first and then to bring that life into reality. We are the co-creators. Now that I told you this secret, you know you have the power inside you to create the life you want.

This is the Key to Your Life and Why You Are Here – to wake up to this truth, realize your own dreams, follow your guidance to self-love and create them along the way. By following my steps and methods, you can achieve that. The time to do it is now and the truth that you already know is in your heart. Just listen. Once you realize this, you will start awakening to your journey and discover the greatest love of all is inside of you.

ENERGY

We are all energy. Everything in the entire universe is made up of energy. Energy never dies, it just changes form. Atoms are made of energy and we are made of atoms. Therefore, we are energy and our thoughts, emotions and feelings are also made of energy. Our thoughts and emotions create things and, in every moment, you're manifesting those thoughts. This is the Universal Law called The Law of Attraction. Once you realize the importance and power of your thoughts and emotions, you can take control of your life. Thoughts become things when you focus your energy on them.

33 SECOND MEDITATION

Sit down and think about what the life of your dreams consists of. No dream is too big or too small! Once you have thought of the life you desire, write it down in detail. Now for 33 seconds, imagine yourself already living the life of your dreams. Visualize being there by touching the trees near you, tasting the food, hearing and smelling the ocean. If you can hold those beautiful thoughts with those emotions, attaching your senses to it, for 33 seconds in your mind (meditation) you will bring that into your life. A lot of famous people have used this technique to bring their dreams into reality. As long as you are in the attitude of gratitude and know in full faith it will be your new reality, you will open new doors to manifest it. That's one part to the key to life. Once you do this step, you will then start your own journey to finding your happiness.

INTERNAL GUIDANCE

Start making the right choices, the ones now presenting themselves to you on your path. Use your internal guidance. If it feels good and comes from love, the answer is yes. If it feels wrong and not good for you in your heart, the answer is usually no. Once you recognize your internal guidance, you can change everything. You can then move forward and make a new decision from your heart because that is where our truth lives. Any obstacles you uncover can be cleared, like clearing a level in a game.

SOUL AND EGO

When I refer to the heart, I also mean *soul* and when I refer to the mind it is referred to as *ego*. These terms go together and bring duality into this world that causes us to feel separate from one another. Step away from your ego self as it will never show you the truth. No two people have had the same experiences, upbringing, or conditioning. Therefore, that reality in your mind is one you made up that will never match the truth of anyone else. No two people are alike, think alike or have walked the same path. Only your heart can match the truth and, if you follow it, you will get everything you always wanted. Know that you need to uplevel your decisions to change your life. Start making new decisions from your heart instead of continuing to make the same decisions from your mind.

KARMA AND REPEATING CYCLES

Sometimes you see repeating patterns in your life that you want to change. When you recognize these patterns, you can see them as a gift. You can choose differently, and stop the karmic wheel from continuing. Choose from your heart! When the same problem arises repeatedly, and is never resolved, you will know this is a lesson. Once you change your perspective and answer from your heart, you will release the toxic energy in your life. You will then resolve everything you see that repeats on your path by asking yourself if it is a sign. To recognize these signs and change them releases your karma in this lifetime. Now you can take control of your own karma.

LIFE PATH

After following your path for some time, you will begin to love yourself. By making different choices from your heart, you will begin taking the journey you were meant to be on, the journey to you. You will be proud of yourself and your accomplishments as you see that you're on the right path to fulfilling your life purpose. You will grow into a person who respects your truth in your heart. You cannot help but love yourself if you know you are making choices from your heart with respect to yourself and others.

Soon we will start to see the changes in the world around us. We are each here to be unique and to love each other's differences and to learn and grow from them. If we follow these steps and always choose from our heart, we will realize that there is much more to life. Once we are all living in self-love, we will then break down all the barriers to our ruling and all that has prevented us from learning our truth.

We create our individual and collective realities because we are all energy. It just takes one person to bring forth these universal truths and realize that we are co-creators manifesting our thoughts and feelings. You can choose to focus on your own dreams and go create them. A positive change in one person's vibration has a ripple effect that will impact our population by shifting our individual and collective energies. Once a certain percentage of the population attains this, it will increase the entire vibrational scale on our planet, bringing positive energy and intentions into the highest energy flow of love. We can change the world we live in. We will then have the most amazing outcome here in our new reality. The one you didn't know could even exist. The one you didn't know you were here to create.

We can have everything by eliminating the lower vibrational energies and toxicity. Once each person shifts their focus of energy onto themselves, we will then shift into a higher dimension, a much higher vibration, and the low vibrational energies will cease to exist and power our reality. This is the key to our ascension. The time is now. We cannot do this alone. Each of us has a part in this life and the new decisions we make will raise our vibration and open new doors to manifesting that reality. All it takes is one small change at a time. Learning to love yourself is one of the most important things we can accomplish in our lives. Once you love yourself, you can then love others unconditionally. We can then help each other eliminate the reality that has become our truth.

SELF LOVE/ACTUALIZATION

In order to live as we always imagined, we must accept all our brothers and sisters as equals and share this message with the world. To get us out of this current world, we must realize our power as co-creators. We must use our thoughts and emotions now to bring our own dreams to life. Once we all stand together in our heart space of self-love and see the love we have in our hearts, low vibrational energy will no longer exist to distract us. One small change will set us free! Our life is here to shift our energy into our hearts and to use our minds to create what our hearts desire.

We all have our own internal guidance in our souls. If you follow your signs, choose differently from your heart, learn lessons on the way, and release karmic/repeating patterns which raise your vibration, you will then find your heart and your truth. We are all co-creators and energy and love is the highest energetic vibration. We can achieve a new perspective and a new positive reality. When we choose from our hearts, we are choosing ourselves. The key in doing all of this is finding out that the truth to life is to love yourself first and then share that love with everyone else.

Linda Creed found self-love and chose to share her wisdom with the world in her song. She learned self-love was the key to unlocking and breaking our limiting beliefs that define who we are. Now you get to decide who you are, who you know to be true in your heart. Focus your own energy on yourself. When each one of us puts our love into ourselves instead of putting love into money and power; only then will the world truly know peace.

Jodi Polen

What If There Is Nothing Wrong With You?

"No problem can be solved from the same consciousness that created it."
~ Albert Einstein

I'm about to tell you something that I didn't always have the courage to say out loud, much less put it in writing for the whole world to see. With time and healing, I am now able to speak about my life from a space of gratitude.

This is my journey. My adventure in re-discovering the joy of living, the joy of having a body and the ways in which pole-dancing contributed to the creation of a life I always knew was possible. When I perceive the energy of who I was as a young child, I get the sense of total freedom, joy, exuberance and ease with my body and my being.

I was 3 years old when my family decided that there was something wrong with me. They decided that I was a problem that needed to be fixed. I was one of those kids who couldn't sit still. I never did what I was told, and I was always saying the things no one wanted me to say. In essence, everything I did was wrong.

I started to believe that there was something wrong with me. This seemed to be the only logical explanation, as I was so different from everyone around me. I began making myself small enough to fit into a tiny little box where I could hide from everyone. With time, I even began hiding from myself. This way of hiding became normal to me.

I figured if I could hide and be what everyone else wanted me to be, that everything would work out. The problem was that no matter how much I hid, no matter how small I made myself, I was still the problem that needed to be fixed.

For the first 30 years of my life I got really comfortable hiding to please everyone who felt uncomfortable around me. I hid behind drugs, alcohol and abusive relationships.

I cut myself off from life and the expression of it with my body. Relationships, work, sex, play – everything was dull. The shutting down of my being began to be reflected through my body. Eventually, I was in total lockdown. My body no longer moved with ease in the world and there was an overall sadness that permeated everything. I knew I was slowly killing myself, that if I kept choosing this path I would die not having done what I came here to do.

A year after I began having this sense, I made the demand to awaken my body, my senses and my being. No matter what it took, no matter what I lost and no matter what I had to change, it had to be done. I knew I had something special to gift to this world and I would not leave without expressing that gift.

I started searching and I met Dr. Dain Heer. He asked me a question that would change my life forever:

What if there is nothing wrong with you?

WHAT? I became aware that what I believed was my greatest wrongness, the ability to see and say what no one else could see and say, was actually my greatest strength.

I began asking myself: "If there is nothing wrong with me, what would I like to create in the world?"

I had been living through what other people wanted me to be. Giving up myself to please everyone else. Giving up myself in order to fit in. Giving up myself so that everyone around me would be happy.

No one had ever asked me what I desired to create. This question opened up a new world of possibilities for me, and I began creating my life the way I had always known was possible. I started laughing, playing, and having fun again.

One of the first things I created in my life were pole-dancing classes. For the first time in 35 years, my body was happy again. The space the classes provided for me to move with my body was priceless. I began to be in complete allowance of the way my body chose to express the caring, kindness, healing and vulnerability of who I truly am in the world.

I knew there was even more to be opened within me. Throughout my healing journey, I became aware of the barriers I was using to block everyone out. I became aware that the only place I allowed myself to express myself fully was in my pole-dancing class.

What would it be like to be this space of me all the time?

Then Tantra came along. Charu, my tantra teacher, held a beautiful space for me to begin exploring what was pleasurable to me. Turns out, after all this time, I had no idea what pleasure was or how to have it! The tantric exercises facilitated the opening of my body and the release of all the energy I was locking in.

In 2012, I created a business that had been hiding deep within me for lifetimes. I took the things that brought me and my body the most joy and I put them together to create something that didn't exist in this reality. Pole Dancing For Consciousness™ became an invitation to a new way of being with the world for everyone who chose it, including me. I went from hiding in a tiny little box to a global business with clients from all over the world.

I've learned that we all have something inside of us that is unique to us. We all have something to gift to the world. A gift that if we don't choose to BE it, the world doesn't get to have it.

What gift are you hiding from the world?

Is now the time to come out and shine?

I'd like to give you my favorite Access Consciousness® tools. You can start using them today to change anything that is not working in your life. I use these simple tools daily to continue out-creating myself. They facilitate me and my clients into creating a life that is beyond surviving and committed to thriving.

TOOL #1: ASKING QUESTIONS AND MAKING DIFFERENT CHOICES

When we function from our minds, we can only create based on what our minds know, which is based on our past experiences. If those past experiences had created what you desired, would you be here right now? I know I would still be hiding in my little tiny box!

Asking questions is about opening the door to new choices and different possibilities. When you ask a question without seeking "the right answer," you allow the Universe to show you the unimaginable.

The unimaginable that goes beyond the mind. Here are my two favorite questions to ask:

What else is possible I haven't imagined?

How does it get any better than this®?

As Albert Einstein said: "No problem can be solved from the same consciousness that created it."

Use these questions to get out of your mind, to open up to more possibilities and into your life!

TOOL #2: FOLLOWING THE ENERGY
Nikola Tesla said: "If you want to find the secrets of the Universe, think in terms of energy, frequency and vibration."

When you begin to ask questions, you have to follow the energy of what is light and expansive for you. When you choose based on the energy of something, rather than your cognitive conclusions, you begin to invite the magic that is available in the Universe to create with you.

What is light and expansive is true for you.

What is heavy and a contraction is not true for you.

Choosing what is light and expansive will always create more for you than choosing based on your mind. Before using these tools, I would choose things that would make others happy. I would choose things because other people wanted me to choose them. Eventually I had created a life that everyone else approved of, but I was miserable!

When I began following the energy, I learned that the Universe always has my back. I learned to trust myself and my awareness. I learned that I am so different from everyone around me – and that's OK! I was able to see me and my capacities and honor what worked for me, beyond what other people wanted for me. I truly began to live my life.

Are you willing to perceive the energy of what will create more for you?

Are you willing to make that demand for you?

TOOL #3: KNOWING THE ESSENCE OF WHO YOU'D LIKE TO BE.

We come into this world full of life, joy and creativity. We choose our families because we know they can't stop us. We choose them because, through them, we can truly see the courage we have to face anything. When I choose to be grateful for my family, I become aware of how much courage it took to live through the abuse I experienced and to create a life beyond it.

In my journey to rediscovering the essence of me, I had to look at every single point of view, judgment, conclusion and decision I'd ever made about myself and everyone around me.

Every time I had a thought, feeling or emotion I would ask these questions:

Who does that belong to?

Who am I being?

If I were truly being me, what would I choose?

I obsessively looked at everything that went through my awareness and slowly peeled off the layers of projections and expectations I'd been living from to find what was truly mine.

I bought my family's points of view as if they were mine. I would behave the way my mother, father, or sister would behave in situations. I had no sense of what was true for me until I began using these questions to clear the energy and open up to the true essence of me.

Today, I continue to ask these questions and I create myself every day! Every day is a new adventure in finding out who I am and opening up to the glorious adventures of life and living.

When you are truly being you, when you trust you and you know you have your own back, the Universe can support you in creating anything you desire. People can show up in your life who actually desire to contribute to you. Everything in your life can change for the better… it always does. You have to choose you first, though.

TOOL #4: INCLUDE YOUR BODY IN THE CREATION OF YOUR LIFE!

Do you know your body functions from total consciousness?

Do you know your body has no judgments… about anything?

Do you know your body can be used as a guide in the creation of your life?

Your body is constantly communicating with you through your senses. You can use all these tools and begin a conversation with your body – as if you were talking to your best friend. Start asking your body questions and follow the energy to what is light and expansive for your body. Here are just a few examples:

Body…

> Are you hungry?

> What would you like to wear?

> How would you like to move?

> What would be fun for you today?

These are the first steps to a journey with your body that can and will transform your life. Ask the questions. Perceive and follow the energy to what is expansive for you and your body. These tools have facilitated me into creating a life that always expands and grows. If you use them, they can contribute to you as well.

My purpose is to empower you to know that you know. You know something that no one else knows, and that can change the world.

Is now the time to BE it?

Patty Alfonso

Your Body –
The Gateway to Your Divinity

"And I said to my body, softly. 'I want to be your friend.'
It took a long breath and replied, 'I have been waiting my whole
life for this'"
~ Nayyirah Waheed

It's 2:00 pm in the afternoon. My 6-year old self is sitting on the floor, my back up against my bed, listening to soft music and writing poetry. I can hear my little voice say, "There must be something wrong with me, to be sitting here all alone, writing to myself and feeling sad." Yet on the flip side, it all felt "right."

As I jotted down my rhythmic thoughts on paper, I worried that someone might find them, so I'd take my paper so artistically encapsulating my innermost deepest thoughts and throw it into the deep abyss of the garbage pail where no one else could find it.

To this day, I wish I had saved those renditions. However, how was I to know then, how valuable they'd be? I was so little, innocent, and naïve that, as I reflect back, I don't even think I knew of the artist I was or that "poetry" or "rhyming" was even a thing. I just know that

I always had a thing for "beauty" and to write my thoughts in this way was to me, pure and utter "beauty."

I may not remember exactly what I was processing in those moments but what I do know is that I felt deeply about everything as a young girl. When I was happy, I was happy and when I was sad, I was sad. The only way to move through these feelings was to write, listen to music and dance my way into pure bliss. I didn't dare talk about my deepest thoughts to anyone. No one would understand. I didn't even understand at times!

Yet, my intuition knew and it was my body that would guide me back to the divinity of who I am through pen to paper or through dancing to the beat of my own soul in a way that felt graceful and enchanting. I didn't know it then but in those moments, I was one with the divine in me. I was home.

And it worked. Every. Single. Time.

Yet I can still remember thinking at times that something must be wrong with me. I was confused. The fact that I liked to be alone, to write or dance by myself with such melancholy, seemed strange. Oftentimes I felt as if I didn't belong or fit in, like in those moments when I'd open my heart to another and they didn't always reciprocate the same back to me. I made that mean something about me, as in, I must not be worthy or lovable. I felt lost and alone many, many times.

Then, one day my little inner genius found a way to belong and feel safe. A way to navigate the world she didn't often understand. She learned how to conform to what others wanted, to be accepted. She realized if she was just the way she knew others wanted her to be then she would fit in and make everyone happy. So, early on she learned how to calibrate herself to the frequency of another and became a master at it.

That little girl became whatever was required: the nice girl, the happy girl, the good girl and even the rebel, the one that knew how to be a misfit when necessary to show she was just as cool as the next person. She didn't like conflict, so she knew instinctively when to stay quiet and simply witness as she allowed others to lead and she would follow.

Yet there was a gift in this that she carried. She was also the little girl who saw the divinity in everyone she met. She had this capacity to love immensely and to take things on, even if they hurt. She'd still see their beauty and deep down acknowledge their pain. Yet this also set her up to feel disempowered, by seeing everyone else as this divine, beautiful being. Again, everyone but herself.

She lost herself along the way. She entered her early adult years as a master in becoming the perfect version of what she thought others wanted her to be and she followed suit. She continued this way of feeling safe in a world that was often cruel and asleep.

105

It seemed to be working, as she didn't know of any other way.

What I then realized over the years of my own awakening was that I was asleep as well, asleep to my own inner wisdom, power and guidance that I knew as a little girl. So much so that in my early teens I slowly strayed from those things that brought me the most joy and beauty, such as dance, writing, and music.

I quit dance because it was "uncool" and none of my friends did it. I quit playing music because that wasn't "cool" either. I even ran out of a drama audition because my friends were laughing at me in the background so hard. And to be ridiculed felt more painful than standing in my truth and beauty.

So, what else was a girl so unsure of herself to do next but to do what she knew how to do best? To follow suit. I began partying and drinking and, as time went on, it became the place I felt most comfortable. I was the life of the party, I made others laugh and, most importantly, I felt good. I felt happy, relaxed and as if I could be anyone I wanted to be!

After college, I coupled partying and drinking with an eating disorder. One thing I thought I could control was my body. Add to that a year-long relationship with drugs – they took me to that happy place. Something I am not proud of; yet it was a significant part of my journey and my awakening. I could give you all the gory details but that's not what's important here.

What is important is that this was a pure symptom of my loss of power and self. My disconnection from my body, my spirit. My years of conforming for others, being the nice girl, the good girl, the rebel or the girl that would no longer allow herself to get angry or sad because it felt too painful, lonely and wrong. The girl who was living with the pain of feeling so much of the world around her, yet didn't know that was what she was feeling, so she opted to feel no longer. The one who lost all her creative vices, those which had served her and the ones she no longer felt she deserved. The one who no longer knew how to just "be" one with herself and her divinity. It felt too painful to be in this body.

Until that one day at a mere 94 lbs., the morning after a binge-drinking, drug-dabbling weekend, I woke up alone, face down on my apartment floor. I tried to get up several times but had no choice except to call 911 on myself. With all my vitals down, it could have been the last day of my life. I not only woke up physically off the floor, but I woke mentally, spiritually, and emotionally as well. My journey had begun.

This was my first awakening towards re-learning who I am: remembering and reclaiming each and every part of me I had lost along the way. This journey is not for the faint of heart. But what I have come to understand now is that it is more beautiful than one will ever know. It's by staying in the familiar, the old, the suffering that we do not allow ourselves to see the beauty in our existence on this journey we call "life."

It's about understanding who we are, our makeup, what makes us thrive and feel alive. There are moments in our life when there will be suffering, struggles and challenges. It's knowing how to move through them that's important.

During the years that followed, I incurred many health repercussions and a significant loss within my family. My body continued to scream at me in ways I will never forget. In ways so painful, I couldn't help but listen. She needed nourishment on the physical, emotional, mental and spiritual level.

I listened.

I ate differently, I danced again, I wrote poetry, and journaled. I surrounded my space with beauty and items that spoke to me, to remind me of who I really am. When I danced, I felt my spirit come alive! I'd move my hips and watch them in the mirror sway to the beat of my heart. I'd feel my body with my fingertips from my thighs to my stomach and up to my chest and revel in the sensuality of my body as she felt most alive. This wasn't easy to get myself to do at first but once I did, it brought me so much joy and reverence for my body again.

Little by little I was healing, finding my way back to myself, my joy, and to the essence of who I am.

Yet this is not about a destination, because my journey didn't end there. It was just the beginning. The beginning of recognizing and embracing my dear, sensitive and empathic body and soul. The one that feels so deeply. The one who holds gifts and revels in the joy of seeing the beauty in others and having it be reflected back to her just the same. The one whose life is now unfolding in ways that are empowering, enlightening and deeply connected to the divinity of who she is and the divinity of the oneness that we all are. The one who now thrives on assisting others on their path of awakening to the divinity of who they are.

There are so many of us sensitive, gifted, soulful, deeply intuitive, empathic souls on this path of awakening and you might be one of them. One who is yearning to find yourself again, to be one with who you are and make your way back home. The one who has been battling with their own self-worth, beauty and power.

I come to you with an invitation to find that home in your body. To understand that your body is the gateway to your divine nature, your joy, beauty, power, and your path to loving yourself unconditionally. We all have initiations, challenges and struggles, and how you choose to move through these moments is what's important.

There is that quote, "To heal is to feel."

It's time to allow your body to guide you, especially in those moments when you feel lost, uncertain and want to stray.

When there is pain that arises, love that pain and get curious about what messages there are for you.

Below are 5 sacred steps to assist you in re-connecting to your body as you continue on your path of awakening to the divinity of who you are!

1) Allow yourself to get curious when uncomfortable emotions or thoughts arise. Choose to be with them rather than distract your awareness away from them. Ask first, "Is this my emotion or someone else's?" Often as sensitive, empathic souls, we can take on the emotions and energies of others. Trust your answer. If it's your feelings, find the root of the emotion by simply closing your eyes and asking questions like, "What am I sad about?" You can do this through movement, sitting in silence, or through writing, pen to paper.

2) Be patient, kind and compassionate with yourself as you allow yourself to feel. Do not judge and allow the emotions to come out in the form that's needed. Ask your body, what she/he needs. Is it to cry, scream, move, laugh? Emotions are "energy in motion" and to release them is a must in order for

healing to occur. Don't hold back. This is a form of self-love even if it doesn't feel like it in the moment.

3) Notice how you feel. Do you feel relief? Acknowledge where you are without judgment and give yourself space to journal with all that comes up for you. See if you can find any golden nuggets to help you understand what caused the emotion in the first place so you know how to move through it in the future.

4) Celebrate yourself for giving yourself this space. What is that thing that brings you the most joy and allows you to feel alive? Let yourself go there to honor your process and bring you back to a place that feels most beautiful to you. You will feel the immediate shift in your body.

5) Get support if needed! This journey is not easy to do on your own. Find a mentor, a friend you trust, or a teacher. But always remember to follow your inner guidance along the way.

Dana Canneto

Strange Magic

Then he said to Thomas, "Put your finger here; see my hands.
Reach out your hand and put it into my side. Stop doubting and
believe."
~ NIV John 20:27

I have always wanted to believe that the magic I witnessed in my dreams was true in reality. I didn't want to live in a world where it wasn't. But I had no proof. Nothing happened with my eyes open. I read the Bible we had in the house, when no one else did. Unbelievable tales were woven in the Bible. One was so important, they started keeping track of time according to it. Why wouldn't the other fantastical things be real?

I strained to break the veil that kept me stuck in this plane. The life where everything was chaos, and there was no real purpose to any of it. They come, they eat, they reproduce, they die. Everything is exactly what it looks like, and there was nothing to see here, so move along. I knew in my heart I was something else, but I was afraid of it, whatever it was. I hated this meat suit I wore and its inability to conform.

They say we keep ourselves from so much by our willingness to believe. Our will makes or breaks the outcome of an event. It effects what you experience. That is unless the Universe has different plans for you, in which case there's nothing even an iron will can prevent. December 31st, 2006 the Universe was to have its way, and the veil was torn. That day I understood the world really is a magical place. Nothing fantastical had ever happened to me in real life, before that day in Calico Ghost Town.

Established in 1881 as a silver mining town, Calico Ghost Town had become a tourist spot on the way to and from Las Vegas. As I was walking down Main Street in Calico, I was hit on the head. Hard! Ooh it gets better. I was wearing a cowboy hat. Then I got the back belt loop of my pants pulled as I was waiting to ride the train holding my daughter's hand. Again no one was around. I went to pick up our old west photos and asked the employee there, "Are there ghosts here? What do they do?" She answers "Oohhh, they touch people on the head and tap them on the back." I was losing my mind I tell you! I had no one to talk to and things just kept on happening.

My self-loathing drove me to starve myself into adrenal fatigue (though I had no name for it until recently). My doctor came up with one test after another, to no avail. Some tests, like the MRI, made me feel like I was the clapper inside of a giant bell, as if every part of my being was vibrating violently. The fatigue was debilitating, and with no medical diagnosis, it probably seemed like I was making it up. The strangest things happened. I could feel electricity. Like the static you feel on TV, but subtler energy.

I visited Denise, a homeopathic professional who muscle-tested me on flower essences. Muscle testing is when you talk directly to the soul. Our soul is the timeless energy within us that knows the lessons it is here on earth to learn and can truly tell you what is happening. Our ego is what we speak from, what filters our experiences and colors our opinions. The ego and soul rarely communicate. I was asked to hold the flower essence of the Bleeding Heart flower. It is in the fuchsia family and resembles a heart with a droplet falling out of the bottom.

I was muscle tested repeatedly. Denise shook her head, saying, "This can't be right," and tested again. I asked what was wrong. "This essence is for when a soul hates the body and is constantly trying to destroy it." I froze. It was like I had been hiding in this darkly lit corner where no one could see me, and suddenly, the light was on. It was 100% true, but how could a plant know that?

I later had Quantum Bio-Feedback done. That's when a very light electric frequency is sent through your body, and read back into a computer program. It yielded similar results, information that should otherwise seem magically derived. The results found 60% abandonment emotionally –how could a computer program read *me*? Call out physical ailments I never discussed with the operator? I really started seeing things then. I not only felt the energy, I saw it: around everything that had life and held energy. It looks like that halo they picture around saints, except it's full-body. You should see the mountains. They just explode with it!

I did have one friend I could ask for help. I had been drawn to her, since I met her in 1996. She just felt so good to be around. I went in one day when I was at my wit's end. "It's OK," she comforted me. "It's just your awakening" her friend added. One thing that has stuck with me that she advised was that, "You can ask how, you can ask when or where, but you can never ask why because it might not be something you're supposed to know." She explained that there was nothing much she could tell me to do or read, but that I should pursue the learning I was drawn to. So, I did.

There were people I became obsessed with – Nickola Tesla, Edgar Cayce, Aimee Semple McPherson, Mary Magdalene –going places they had been, and finding hidden information about them was like a religious experience. I'm not sure why them. I don't ask. I began reading all sorts of esoteric and scientific things, anything that blew my dress up. Spiritualism, Magic, Rosicrucians (a spiritual movement from 17th Century Europe), Science, Geography, even the magazine, Fortean Times. Some seemed utter gibberish while others were Universal Truths, like prime numbers in nature. I was learning to trust my feelings and follow them even if I didn't understand why.

As afraid as I was of myself, I was more afraid of the beast that stalked me, or rather the suffering it would cause anyone who loved me. Multiple Sclerosis was the diagnosis they gave my mother at 31 years of age, one year after what they thought was a stroke that caused total temporary paralysis on the right side of her body. I was only 7 when it happened, and I knew it was hereditary. At age 12, I learned breast cancer was hereditary, from my Dad's cousin who was going through treatment. She told me quietly, apart from the family, showing me the tattoos they gave her to line up the laser for treatment. I had decided I wasn't going to be anyone's burden, I was going to suffer alone.

But the Universe was determined to show me love, even if I didn't think I deserved it. I was 16 and my first true love told me he loved me the very first week we were together. Surely you can't be serious? Do you see what I could become? Five years later, when he asked me to marry him, I took to burning myself with a glue gun. No one could possibly want me. He said he would take care of me if any of those hereditary things ever arrived, and he was true to his word.

So, when I was diagnosed in 2012 with breast cancer, the beast had arrived, and now it was time to battle. When I sat alone for the first time, truly feeling the effects of chemotherapy, I asked mentally "What is this all for?"

The answer, from that still small voice was, "You will not be all that changed, but you will change people with what happens to you." After that I had a mission to complete. I was handed a cosmic purpose. That thing I felt I was supposed to be doing, that was previously unknown, was here. I blogged my experience, to keep it fresh in case I ever wanted to revisit it. Carrying all of that learning with me, I started to see connections between things, almost like fishing wire tacked onto this person and that experience. "Enmeshed thinking" they call it. I began attending support meetings for breast cancer survivors. People talked about their lumps and how their husbands didn't touch them anymore. What made me feel differently about my body after treatment? "What did you do to me?" I asked my husband. Better still, "How do we create this change in others?"

We came up with a plan: fundraiser, at first for another organization, before we became our own. We asked 11 breast cancer survivors to become pinups for a calendar to promote body positivity and self-love after diagnosis. They came from all different parts of the United States to participate. We asked photographers I had met doing hobby modeling to take the pictures, wrangled hot rods from our friends, and made up the rest. Haus of Volta finally had a purpose! The name is derived from my background in fashion design. Collaboratives often call themselves "houses" (Haus). Plus my affinity for energy and science gives a nod to Alejandro Volta, the first to measure energy and harness it in a battery.

The saying, "Find a way, and where there is no way, make one," seems to be our *modus operandi*. What started as a yearning to help others like myself overcome their insecurities, has blossomed. Classification barriers exist in the breast cancer community just as they do anywhere else, but they have no weight at Haus of Volta. Regardless of age, stage, race, reconstruction, sexual orientation or identity, all experiences are real and valid. We have been able to get 501(c)(3) nonprofit status, and provide care packages for those affected (discussing sexual dysfunction, cannabis for pain and PTSD, beautiful lingerie for breast cancer patients, and support groups locally). We were able to speak at the University of Southern California and at The Young Survival Coalition Summit 2017.We were also hand-selected by the California Breast Cancer Research Program to be trained in grant writing and to do research officially!

Being asked to walk in New York Fashion Week 2018 for Anaono Lingerie, at 5'9" and 225lbs, was not only a validation of my work but has helped me embrace my larger than life status. Change is the only constant and our current focus is on becoming death doulas. Mentoring many metastatic (incurable) cancer warriors I have found that when support is most needed, loved ones are distant and friends disappear.

I have been inspired to assist a dear friend embrace life, by conquering her fear of death. We are working together to plan her funeral, her way. And we will create a Death Cafe type environment for anyone who wants to talk openly about death and the funerary process. Fear is logical. Faith is illogical. However, letting go of what you may understand to be true has been proven to improve mortality. Our beliefs have real life consequences.

Magic isn't what you think it is. It's not as simple as movies make it out to be. It's complicated, not easily seen, and even harder to believe. The older we get, the less willing we are to try, because for X amount of years it's been a struggle to even exist in this world. Facts cloud our imagination, so full of hereditary odds and statistics. Our minds are wired in both worlds: creative and logical, belief and proof. Blindly depending on just one creates universal unbalance. There are things you want, but it's not time yet. A sequence of events must occur before that thing is made real, before you believe you are capable, and the experience and knowledge is there for the execution. A painter always paints themselves, they say. Believe in your capability and be shown the proof.

Stori Nagel

Uncover Your Authentic VOICE To Heal Your Life

"You must Tune-In to Rock it Out, Woman!"
~ Christine Miskinis

My story has transformed the lives of others. It is my intention that you'll hear your voice through the sharing of mine. Listen closely. My life began during my second decade of life. It came with what seemed to be a death sentence at the time. For a young woman who had already tasted the sweetness of success in her life at the age of 24, I still had so much ahead of me.

I had so much to look forward to, yet my life leading up to that moment was filled with lots of questions, lots of finding my way within boxes, compromises, expectations and societal beliefs about what was possible for someone like me as a single, independent, young woman living on the East Coast of the United States. I found myself teetering between the messages of, "Anything is possible as long as I put my mind to it!" and, "First create security by earning an education, a career with tenure and the love, protection and income of a man." I was also teetering between the thoughts of pursuing my passions of being on stage through performance and teaching in an educational system with a great pension.

I didn't have any answers at the time, yet dreamed of the day when I would have the stability in my life to discover those for myself. I was so on fire about life and passionate about my dreams, but I was most focused on checking off all the boxes so I could be accomplished and become someone of value and worth.

Add to that finding a partner, getting married, and having my first baby before the age of 30, which was a lot to consider, as a young woman finding her way in the world. Just so you have a better idea of what my days looked like, they were filled with working full time, tutoring after school for extra money, exercising to keep fit, socializing with friends and spending a good deal of my time with my boyfriend. At night I would fit in my passion for theater and auditioning while studying for more degrees so that I could increase my income and keep my job. Behind the scenes, my life consisted of rushing off from one thing to the next, feeling exhausted, feeling uncertain, and not knowing what to do about that.

Take a moment here to ask yourself, Where are you giving away your own power? Are you still living within others' expectations or rules? Who is holding your self-worth?

It was no surprise to me that I would find myself in the office of a gastroenterologist dealing with life-threatening results. I hadn't felt well for most of my life. Although I always loved food and had a healthy appetite, it was difficult for me to digest.

Since the age of five I'd struggled with dehydration, constipation, and stomach upset. At any moment I would eat something that would send me into a "stomach attack" which lasted for the duration of my childhood into adulthood. There were no answers other than that I had a sensitive stomach and a case of irritable bowel syndrome. I was taking medication but I didn't feel any better. In fact, it seemed as though it was getting worse.

As a schoolteacher, I would find myself having to get someone to watch my class while I ran off to the bathroom for a long period of time. While I was out with my friends, I would have to excuse myself after taking just a few bites of my meal to be sick in the bathroom. While I didn't hide this from anyone, it wasn't something that you would know about me unless you were close enough for me to share it with you or for you to be in my presence as it happened.

So, I carried on with life, doing all that I knew to do, eating as best as I could, exercising, and not giving too much time or attention to the problem. My friends were shocked to learn about what was happening to me behind closed doors! They were appalled at my quality of life. They said things like, "I would never know that you're dealing with this. You're always happy and smiling!" This was true, for the most part. I'm the type of person who sees the world as a glass half full. I'm optimistic and passionate about fulfilling my goals and desires.

Yet at what cost does that come? At what point do I say I am my own authority? At what point do I finally start to listen to my inner voice?

In retrospect, I see how I was not worthy of my own attention. I was doing a great job at keeping busy, being productive, and surviving life. Or so I thought, until this moment. Let's travel back to 15 years ago when I was suffering from awful stomach episodes that would happen sometime late in the middle of the night. I was living alone at the time and would suddenly wake up with burning sensations deep inside my belly. My stomach would feel tight, the pain would increase, along with the churning noises of all gastric juices and horrific cramps!

I would immediately be doubled over and find myself crawling on the floor, unable to stand, unable to straighten my spine, trying everything in my power to make it stop with no avail for 14-16 hours uninterrupted! I often ended up lying on my bathroom floor depleted, or in the emergency room, where I was given antacids and told there was nothing else that could be done, or that I'd have to wait until it passed.

One day after having multiple tests and biopsies, I walked into my doctor's office to hear the results. "Christine, we have some troubling news. The biopsy shows you have something called Barrett's Esophagus, which is a disease from a lifetime of digestive issues. As a result of years of acid reflux, your stomach lining starts to grow up into your esophagus to protect it but anytime there is abnormal cellular growth it is pre-Cancerous."

I could feel my body tense up and a wave of nausea overcame me. "Okay doctor, what now? What can we do to treat this? What is the procedure on medication that I can take at this time?"

"Well, you are in the pre-Cancerous stage, which means we are unable to treat it, but when it becomes Cancer we will go in and…"

Everything went quiet in the room. As I desperately searched my doctor's eyes for answers, I was met with a blank stare and given information about what could possibly come next. In that moment, I started thinking back on what I had been experiencing all my life, and connecting that to what I knew of Cancer, which was a death sentence at the time. I could suddenly feel the fear and panic setting in and then this happened: an enormous amount of energy filled up from inside my body, like a hand fills a glove.

It was as if my soul sat up from inside of me. Everything got quiet and I heard a calm, clear voice say, "Go off, and allow your body to heal! All is well."

For whatever reason, I was calm. It was as if I was hearing the voice of God, but it was the sound of my own inner voice. A new feeling of peace and trust filled me. I left the doctor's office that day knowing that my body would heal itself. While I didn't have the answers, I had faith that I would figure it out, and that I would live.

What's most important for you to know is that during that moment in the doctor's office, I had a Spiritual Awakening and a moment of divine truth – which is that "I am responsible for my life – body, mind, and spirit." This meant it was time to pay attention to me. It was time that I became my own authority. It was time that I started to listen to my own Inner Voice and live my life connected to my higher self. In just a few days, after having had this experience, a friend of the family reached out to me and said he knew of a holistic nutritionist who could help me heal my body. I knew this was my lifeline. This was my next step in recovering myself and caring for my body.

The true miracle came a few months later when I returned to the doctor for more testing. He came into the room and told me my esophagus had scar tissue which meant it was healing, and there was no more new, cellular growth! I tried sharing what I had been doing for those months since that day I was given the diagnosis, but my doctor informed me that if I was not going to take the prescription, he was unable to continue to treat me. He explained that in medical school he had learned to prescribe medication that would assist in managing and healing disease. While I understood and had great respect for his learning, I knew that his truth was not my own. Another lesson in and of itself. I left the doctor's office that day, never needing to return. So began the next phase of my Awakening which was to share what I'd discovered with the world by becoming a Transformational Life Coach!

These are the concepts I invite you to consider in creating a life that you love, which starts by first, Loving Yourself.

1) Nutrition:

Could food be the gateway into your own connection to our world? Can it provide physical and emotional healing? I fell in love with nutrition, the idea of food as medicine and the simplicity that came with nourishing my body. I discovered that the more whole foods I ate, the more organic food I digested and the more water I drank, the more in touch with nature and the world I became! By eating real food, I discovered a greater sense of connection and belonging. Yes, predominately eating food from the earth can bring you healing and higher states of consciousness. All my senses were heightened, including being able to hear the voice of my intuition.

2) Reclaim your Power by Trusting your Intuition (inner voice):

This means becoming your own authority. You can do this by listening to your intuition: that inner voice which is a direct connection to God, source and the universe. Trust yourself by building that trust through honoring your word. You will trust yourself more and more as you continue to fulfill your own commitments. This takes creating the space to be still and to listen. It also requires that you act on the guidance that you receive with faith and unwavering confidence. Life will expand to meet you at the capacity that you trust and honor yourself. You can start tuning in with just 3-5 minutes each morning. Sit quietly and ask one question for that day and then listen for words, emotions, and visions. Then take action!

3) Speak your Truth:

The first stage of being in integrity is honoring your word to yourself. How you spend your time and what you give your attention to shows what you're committed to. This will lead to your results. Honoring your boundaries puts structure into what you're creating. This includes your mind. Be mindful of the thoughts you are thinking, what you are listening to and the company that you keep. Learn to build up the confidence to Speak your Truth.

Love Revolution

Remember, you can only love others to the degree at which you love yourself. It is not selfish, it is self-preserving. Start fostering your worth, follow your inner guidance, and become your own Authority by Speaking your Truth.

This is the Love Revolution, and should you feel inspired to receive additional support, I am here!

Christine Miskinis

Love Revolution

Kerala Dreams:
An Indian American Woman's Experience

"People do not succeed because they're better than others; they succeed because they create a path for themselves and stay focused."
~ Susan Kokura

June in Kerala was always an interesting time, with monsoon breaks, tons of rain, and small glimpses of blaring sunshine where I would run outside to play whenever I had the chance. "Don't go too far," my Amma (mother) would yell from inside the house. I'd run barefoot to the Periyar River which flowed along the back of our house, and float my carefully designed paper boats. As I watched them set sail, I dreamed of one day traveling far away to see my Achachen (father).

Achachen went to America in 1988 to set up a new life for us and when the time came, he would send for us to join him there. Every day, as time got closer to us leaving for America, I dreamed of big houses and lots of people with an overabundance of money, food, and clothing. I imagined that everyone would be extremely happy to meet me, similar to the two lovely ladies from England I had met when we went to get our paperwork to go to America. They had the most gorgeous white skin and offered me a piece of Big Red Gum.

In my dreams, the people in America were all white with rosy cheeks like Alice in Alice in Wonderland. They all had their pick of any job they wanted to do, and could follow their hopes and dreams. I thought life was going to be so easy. We would no longer have to struggle with having enough food in the house and we could have all the beautiful clothes I'd ever wanted instead of the same two dresses I wore consistently. My mother wouldn't have to work so much and take care of my Velyammachi (grandmother) and my two sisters by herself. My father would have so much money stored up, we wouldn't need to do anything.

The telegram came that morning on June 22, 1989 from my father in America that he was ready to have us join him. All our family and friends came to say goodbye as we left with joy. I was 8 years old then, a scared, shy, little girl holding onto my mom's sari, getting on that plane from Kerala, India. As the plane took off from Cochin airport, I knew life would never be the same. We arrived at JFK airport on June 24, 1989. My picture perfect utopian America ended up giving me fear, loneliness and anxiety when we arrived here.

Where were all the white people?

Love Revolution

When we landed at the airport, there were so many colors of people with different accents. I thought we were somewhere else, and the plane had redirected us to another country. No one told me, or I had never learned that America is the "melting pot."

The first shocker was the language. I couldn't understand anything and couldn't communicate. What were all these people saying? Then my father picked us up in his silver Chrysler all by himself, lifting our entire luggage with zero help. Then my dream of the big home was burst by a tiny, one-bedroom apartment above a storefront for all of us to share in a 3-block, predominately Caucasian town called Waldwick in New Jersey. This was definitely not what I had envisioned. There was no one there except my parents and my siblings.

We had our cousin who lived in the same town with his family and that is how my dad had discovered this wonderful tiny town. He had a Chinese restaurant in town, Hunan Garden, where we all helped. I even remember stuffing eggrolls into the paper sleeves and answering the phone. The only English phrase I knew was "Hunan Garden, May I help you?" Knowing just that sentence wasn't going to help, so I was placed in an English As a Second Language (ESL) class in school. Growing up here was so hard, living a double life as an Indian and an American.

Let me walk you through the feelings of an immigrant in the first few years, from my personal experience. The beginning is lonely, and you feel isolated. You've uprooted your life from a place you were very familiar with, always surrounded by people you knew, to a country where you don't know many people. Feeling empty for the first year, you can't really tell where the loneliness comes from.

Since my father came one year before us, he found a church community. Every Sunday we would attend. That was our big family outing every Sunday morning, to go to our Syrian Orthodox Christian Indian church in Rockland County. There were enough people to socialize with on Sundays, but the deeper emotional connection took some time to build. In the beginning, surrounding yourself with those with a similar in culture is important. The Indian immigrant communities help foster that feeling of belonging. Getting involved in cultural events in the community helps meet other immigrants going through similar struggles.

We were the typical Indian family with blue collar working parents. My father was a machinist and my mother worked as a dietary aide in a nursing home. This was extremely difficult for her because, back in India, she was a teacher. My two older siblings were still in high school when we came here and right away they had to find jobs waitressing and working as a cashier at the local grocery store to help support the family.

I cannot stress enough that childhood and growing up was hard here. We struggled just like any other immigrant family: financially, culturally, trying to assimilate to an unknown culture, and trying to deal with stereotypes. Being only one of the handful of brown-skinned kids in school was tough. It was hard trying to defend against all the stereotypes of Indians growing up. Let me give you some examples. All Indians aren't from one place, and we don't all speak Hindi. I am a Christian, not a Hindu by religion.

My last name isn't Patel and I definitely did not win the spelling bees. I am not amazing at math, nor did my parents work at a 7/11, a call center, with engineering, healthcare or in information technology. Sometimes I did smell of curry if my mom cooked Indian food at home, and sometimes I am still late to places (Indian standard time). I am definitely beyond Bollywood! I don't dress up in Indian clothes every day or walk around with a red dot on my forehead. Being able to brush off stereotypes and discrimination is important. Not everyone is going to like you and that is OK.

As I grew older, I realized I am a multicultural Indian-American woman. At first, I was like a secret James Bond-type spy, leading a double life. I mastered the art of handling my double life pretty well, switching back and forth between languages and keeping it all separated. Whenever I was around Indians or large Indian American communities, I would step into a whole different world where I had more conversations in Malayalam, and I could sip on a cup of chai and listen to Indian music. When I was around my American friends, I would only speak English, would hide my Indian clothes, blast English-only music, spray a ton of perfume to cover up the smell of curry, order takeout so no one had to eat my mom's cooking and would tell my parents to speak the minimal English they knew to my friends.

I was so embarrassed to be Indian and spent so much energy hiding my heritage and trying to be American. I felt like I was forced into being someone I wasn't. Sometimes, feeling like you are two different people can be difficult.

I decided to go away to college to pursue a doctorate in pharmacy; I was the only one in my family who had the opportunity to go to a university for higher education. At college, I wanted to have nothing to do with Indian people; I had only American friends and roommates. I would be friendly with the Indian students, but not get too close. I spent 6 years in Philadelphia and put myself through school, working numerous part time jobs, living off Costco samples in a tiny nostril of a bedroom in West Philadelphia.

I even went so far as to get an arranged marriage at age 23 because I thought it was the right thing to do, being Indian, and it turned out to be a complete failure which led to a divorce. I couldn't relate to my spouse because he was raised in India and I was raised in America.

After the divorce I felt as if I had the scarlet letter in the Indian communities I once felt comfortable in. I fell into a deep depression for several years, isolating my family and friends, who couldn't understand what had gone wrong. I turned to a lifestyle of partying and drinking and seeking comfort in loveless relationships where I felt no self-worth. One day when my life hit rock-bottom, I realized it could only go up from there and I decided to turn my life around. Life is a one-time offer; I didn't want to waste it. I built back my life one brick at a time to create a strong foundation of self-love, strength, courage, and faith. You don't need the approval and validation of others.

But you know what I wish someone had told me back then? I want to share with you this information: you don't have to switch between two identities. You can be both Indian and American. There is an opportunity, which I realized later, for a beautiful cultural exchange. You can blend the two cultures of your life and many other cultures you are exposed to and create your own identity. You just educate those around you to give other people the tools to understand your identity.

One thing I did learn over the years is that no matter what culture you are, no matter how difficult life becomes, always remember to love yourself. Self-love is so important. Today I stand as a strong, successful woman who is fearless about what life has to bring. I embrace my Indian culture by wearing the clothes and jewelry, eating and cooking the food, listening to the music and celebrating the holidays with family and friends. Always keep an open mind and get to know people from all different cultures. You can learn so much from every culture.

Fast forward in time. Recently, I had an older Indian woman who just arrived from India tell her two daughters, "Look, she's an Indian author and a pharmacist. Girls, I want you to meet this amazing woman. Did you know she came here when she was a little girl and now she works in a big hospital in New York City and writes books? Look what she's made of herself today!" The woman bragged to her kids, and then said, "Go ahead, Susan, tell them how you became so successful."

I paused for a moment. I had never thought about it. I was mortified with embarrassment. To this day, I still do not know how to take these types of comments. It must be my Indian side. How did I get to where I am today? That was a really tough question to answer. When people talk about Indians, they think success. Success doesn't come overnight. It comes from the values of hard work and humility, and from wise investments and living below one's means.

So, what are the values of an immigrant coming to an unknown land like the United States? Definitely for me the important traits that stand out are living below your means, hard work and humility.

No job is beneath you. I have gone from working in libraries dusting shelves, to cleaning people up in nursing homes, to being a cashier at a grocery store, taking care of the elderly, cleaning bathrooms, bartending, working in various stores as a clerk, to housekeeping, to pharmacy technician, to pharmacist, to college professor, to corporate manager, to running my own business, to being a mother.

Each job worked as a stepping stone to the next. People do not succeed because they're better than others; they succeed because they create a path for themselves and stay focused.

Always commit to creating for yourself the support you crave. You don't always have to have the same interests or the same background as others. Just be yourself and have patience. I love that I have the power to create the life that I want. I have the power to choose the positives of so many cultures in this country and create a culture of my own.

I feel that I am a powerful, courageous, and loving woman who came from poverty to working my way up to a life I truly love with so many opportunities that continue my path of success. If I fail, I fail forward. Taking away the lessons from my mistakes only makes me stronger. I continue to let go of the past and live and enjoy the moment.

Five years ago, I couldn't even imagine being an author, being comfortable enough to share my experiences. But today I am so blessed to have the opportunity to help others.

I realized I am stronger than I thought I was. All storms eventually pass, and you rise above your circumstances. You have the power within you to rise above anything that seeks to bring you down.

Susan Kokura

Rising Above

"Forget not that the earth delights to feel your bare feet
and the winds long to play with your hair."
~ Kahlil Gibran

It was in the spring of 2015 that I was bathed in the magical knowing that love, love, love is the only REAL energy, the only truth, the only thing that is left when you take away everything else.

Think about it – what if you took away all the physical, the need to clothe, shelter and feed your physical self? What if you no longer had any need to make money, to work, to achieve in this physical world? Nothing to protect or maintain. You were just YOU. Infinite, pure energy and light, free YOU.

For instance, when you're dreaming, do you have to worry about having enough money to do what you want to do in your dream? No. You are just pure consciousness. I imagine this nonphysical reality to be a bit like that: imagination times a million! In that kind of state, what would you be afraid of? What could get injured? What could you lose? Nothing. So, what would you do? LOVE. Imagine what you love, create what you love, go to what you love.

It's funny that this came to me in 2015 because I was "single" for the first time in my life—having walked away from a 700-acre ranch, a brand new home that had my imprint on every interior inch, and as much financial "security" as one could ever need.

Alone, renting for the first time in decades, and stripped of my "assets," I found myself bathed in unconditional, limitless, infinite LOVE. THIS was my Love Revolution!

By the end of this chapter, I believe that YOU are also going to know that love is really the truth around everything. It's absolutely the foundation of everything we do.

And here's the thing, we are here in this physical reality with things we have to do to maintain and protect ourselves. Fear is a very real force, knocking on the door of our consciousness daily. What is an Infinite Being to do down here in this dense, physical reality?

That's the clue: HERE. We came here very intentionally. HERE is Earth. Earth is gorgeous, abundant, bountiful, diverse, majestic, and alive. Mother Earth wants to be your partner in this dance. It is a dance between your physical and infinite self. How do you dance with Mother Earth (one might ask)?

You get to know her. You develop a relationship with Mother Earth through her elements. In this chapter, you are going to weave into your "reality" a whole new way of dancing with this physical reality. I'm really excited to share with you exactly how to begin.

I'm going to encourage you to create an elemental altar in your home, for each of the four elements : air, fire, water, and earth. These altars can be simple. To the casual observer they may just look like a collection of special things that you have arranged on your bedside table or the kitchen windowsill.

We are each being called to sever any idea of, or illusion of separation, and working with the four elements is going to help weave you back into the fabric of Mother Earth, of Gaia.

The first element we start with is AIR, and that is in the direction of the east, or the rising sun. When you create your home altars, as I'm suggesting, you want to create an altar to the element of air in the east. Think about where the sun shines into your home in the morning. That is the east side of your home and the new home of your air altar.

Air is an element that wants to support you in the mental realm. It is represented and symbolized by the breath. Clearly you can connect to the element of air just from breathing deeply.

Connect to your breath now. Breathe deeply so you can hear your breath inside. Imagine your whole body as Mother Earth and allow the breath to come through your own caverns and crevasses. Allow the air to blow away old stories, old energy, and to breathe in new inspiration, new ideas. If you're ever feeling stuck, you can connect to the air element to reinvigorate you.

Air is the intellect. It is the element of communication. You can ask air for the words, or the ideas, that will serve your highest and greatest good as you go through your day. When you do that, you detach from this feeling of being alone, or the attitude that, "I have to figure it out. I have to perform." You are weaving your consciousness into the expansiveness of the Earth around you.

Air travels around the planet, circulating through our own bodies, through the trees, and through the ocean. Your breath is interwoven with the fabric of this planet and is breathed in and out by each person, at some point or another. Air can connect you to this expansiveness. You can close your eyes and maybe imagine yourself flying through the air, getting that higher perspective. It can help you to rise above a difficult situation or misunderstanding.

What to place on your air altar? Think about what you associate with the element of air. The winged creatures are great pieces to have in your elemental altar for air. Crystals or stones that are connected to the mental realm, the higher chakras, are wonderful to have on your air altar. Having a light or a candle is also, of course, really beautiful.

Now we move to the south and the element of fire. Think about the south side of your home. This is where it's the hottest. It's where you might have to have a curtain to keep your home from getting too warm in the middle of the day. In the winter, the sun beams through the windows in the south.

Fire is the element of transformation and inspiration. It's that fire in your belly. It's your sacred spark. It's what gets you fired up. It is also represented by the energy of creative destruction. Think of a forest fire. Forest fires are a natural part of the cycle because they burn away the smaller, or weaker, trees so that the healthy ones can grow bigger and stronger. It also keeps the forest healthy so that when a wildfire does come through, the land doesn't go up in flames like a tinderbox.

Think about how this is reflective of something in your life right now. Where has something "natural" in you been squelched or ignored? And what are some ways you can begin to bring that part of you back into balance? When we connect to these elements we can access natural wisdom that is simply TRUTH.

Fire wants to help you clear away that which is no longer serving you. We want to encourage you that no matter what you've experienced in the past, it doesn't have to determine your present or your future. You can allow fire to burn away the "dead wood," burn away what's clogging, stifling or smoldering your sacred spark. Let fire help you, whether that's building a fire or going into meditation and connecting to fire.

In the era of separation that we're coming out of right now, we've been led to believe that we're separate and we're here to control, manipulate, and take from the Earth, rather than understanding that we're in this very loving relationship.

Mother Earth is called Mother Earth for exactly the same reason that our mothers want to nurture and encourage and love us. Right? That's what she wants to do. She's whispering to you right now. "Give me your old stories, your limiting beliefs, your worries, your fears. Allow me to burn them away to create space for what is possible."

You can go to your fire altar and send into that space whatever you want to release. There are animals associated with the fire altar. One of my favorites is the lion, or the lioness. The serpent, or the snake, is another animal that you can work with in fire. Think of the snake shedding its skin. And then there are stones, such as the tiger's eye, to have on your fire altar. Of course, you want to have a candle and things that inspire you and get you fired up.

There are no rules around creating your altars. What I love about creating them is that you can literally just put a candle in each of those directions in your home and then allow what wants to come to your altars to be attracted to you.

Now we move to the west, the setting sun, and the element of water. For any of us who've ever had the gift of watching the sun set into the ocean, this can be a visual for you. Water is one of my favorite elements. I am a water sign. I'm a Cancer. You might connect to the element of your astrological sign – if you don't know just Google it. Water is the element of emotions. I don't know, but have any of you been feeling any kind of emotional rollercoaster lately? Life is super intense.

Mia Saenz teaches her clients and talks in her book "Mirror Mirror" about "deep pocket moments." Pocket moments happen when you're feeling so great and then all of the sudden you think, "What is going on? I am stuck, what am I even doing? Nothing's working out."

Right? That is where you are being called to connect to water and identify with your emotional realms. Right now, close your eyes for a moment and picture a body of water. What body of water comes to you? Is it a raging river? An ocean? Is it calm or super wavy and turbulent? Maybe you picture a lake or a pond or stream?

Now, ask what wisdom this water wants to share with you right now. Our emotions can cause some tumultuous experiences or feelings in our life. All of us have watched a raging river or been in the ocean and had the waves suck us under. Water is a powerful force. Our emotions can create the feeling of being out of control, gasping for air, or we can learn to allow our emotions to inform us and guide us.

Clara Pinkola Estes, in her book "Women who Run with the Wolves," (Ballentine Books, 1992) compares our creative lives to a river. She says that it is always there, whether it is being allowed to flow, clean and pure, or whether it is polluted, clogged and dammed. We can look at any element of Earth, anything that's catching your eye outside, and connect to the symbolism, the message for you right now.

The land wants to teach you something about you, your natural self. Imagine how many of you can connect to the feeling of being a river that just wants to flow and meander and nurture everything around it, but yet, you've been channeled into a different direction because it was more productive or practical or logical or safe. And you really just want to flow. You want to flow and be your natural, authentic self. See what I mean?

The ocean is the energy of expansiveness. We've been taught a very linear process of living. Step one, step two, step three. If "this" happens and "this" happens then "this" should happen. As an alternative, we could understand the infinite matrix that's all around us at every moment. The elements that are sparking around you, dripping on you and breathing into you, wanting to support you.

What do you need right now? What do you want?

Do you want more support? Do you want more inspiration? Do you want new strength? Do you want the courage to follow your heart?

Connect to what it is you want right now, and you will understand which element will best support your next steps.

Right now, connect to where you're sitting and we will ground in the energies of the element of EARTH. Feel into wherever you are sitting and then connect to the fact that what you're sitting on is being supported by the floor, which is being supported by the Earth under you.

And then move your awareness out to the space all around your home or wherever you are right now, and connect to everything that's growing – the trees, the grass, the flowers, the rivers flowing through, the mountains rising up. Earth is the element of support, of manifestation, of abundance.

Connect to your garden right now. Think about your garden and what you desire, what you want in your life right now. Imagine your dreams growing into fruition just like planting a seed and watching it grow. The Earth element may be the one where you are able to go and release all the limiting beliefs or the negative stories and bury them in the Earth. It's the shit, it's the compost. Mother Earth is like, "Give it to me and I will transmute it into new growth." Don't hang onto it. It gets stinky. Right? Send it into the Earth and allow her to transform it so that you can grow from it rather than feel weighed down by it.

Maybe sometimes you feel the desire to be supported more completely? Have you ever not felt supported?

"I'm not feeling supported so I'm going to spend five minutes to connect to the energy I desire. I'm going to feel myself. I'm going to send my energy, my awareness, down into the Earth. I'm going to connect to how completely massive this energy is, just the expansiveness of the rock and the crystals and the fire and the water and the caverns, and in the iron crystalline core of Mother Earth, how that's all supporting me and loving me."

You come out of that three- or five-minute earth mediation and you feel supported. You're able to move forward with Earth supporting you.

You feel the difference? Earth is in the north. It's the dark side of the home. This is, traditionally, the realms of the ancestors of ancient wisdom. You think of how the indigenous wisdom is coming back right now. The elements are a sign. The way we're following the moon cycles is another sign.

About five years ago, seven years ago, ten years ago, there was hardly anything being shared to such a broad audience about the new moon, or the full moon. Now it is. We're all being called to remember this ancient, indigenous wisdom and that wisdom lives in the element of earth in the direction of the north.

Your elemental altar can create space for you to go to. "I want to feel more supported," so you go and sit in front of your elemental earth altar and connect to that.

The elements are all around you and within you. The air is your breath. The fire, the synapses firing in your brain, the heat generated by your body. The water is the blood, circulating through every cell of your being, and the earth is your skin and your bones, the physical form.

A lot of us feel like we're on a spiritual journey and it can get really expansive up in the stars and the cosmos, right? It can be hard to really be present down here on this planet, because there's so much density. There are so many problems. There is so much crying out for our love. There is so much fear and we want to escape, just float and float away.

And the reason you are here in this physical body is because your soul, your spirit, your light, your energy wanted to come down and play in this beautiful, magical, physical realm. This sensual space where we get to feel and touch and get dirty and get burned and get wet and then remember that we are also the stars.

You are the perfect union of Heaven and Earth. As you connect to the spiritual realm and balance that with this deep reverence and connection and love for Mother Earth, you recover the essence of you who are.

You are matter, made, inspired, illuminated by the energy from above. Where Heaven and Earth meet is you in your heart.

Whitney Freya

Crossroads

*"Everything in life is constantly moving and changing.
Life is about embracing this change, for this change
is the only sure thing in life"*
~ Mimi Ikonn

It was mid-August 2004, when my sister Marla and I decided to take a trip to Tel Aviv. It was time to check up on an investment I had made in a wellness clinic and I wanted to meet the man who had captured my sister's attention enough so that she began to speak and act differently. I also thought it would be a good time to reconnect with her. Over time, our relationship had become estranged. I felt distant, I didn't understand her anymore. They say that behind every fear lies a wish. I feared I was losing my sister and my wish was to be re-connected. I longed for this connection. Little did I know where that connection would lead. Her relationship with Oron began in 2001/02 and from the moment they met things were different.

Marla also had her own hopes for the trip. She was dating Oron who was also running the wellness clinic and was excited for us to meet. We arrived at the airport in Tel Aviv, where Oron was waiting to pick us up.

As I walked up to his car I had a strange feeling come over me. The moment I took my seat, I instantly felt a pain in my stomach and couldn't speak, as if that was ever even possible. My funny, open, talkative personality had suddenly taken a back seat, and I knew in my gut, something was not right.

As we drove away to go to Oron's apartment, my sister kept looking back at me in disgust, as though I was doing something on purpose. She attempted to create dialogue between Oron and me but it just didn't work. Oron made an effort to get to know me by using humor or asking questions but my intuition told me not to trust this man.

After several days with no progress in forming a relationship, this was made explicitly clear to me by my disappointed sister. "How can you be so selfish and inconsiderate?! All he wants to do is get to know you! The least you can do is respond," she complained. Despite her pleas, I felt hesitant about opening up to him and knew my uncertainty about his character prevented us from understanding each other. I wanted it to work, but I just couldn't put my finger on what it was that I was feeling about him. I needed clarity. During this time, we visited the clinic. It was beautiful, just the way I had imagined.

Two days later, late in the evening while driving around Tel Aviv, Oron decided that we could cross the border to spend a few days camping with the gypsies in Sinai, Egypt. When we crossed the border into Sinai, the roads were pitch black; we couldn't see a thing. We arrived at our campground and got ready for bed. As I closed my eyes, I wished that things would improve between the three of us and finally put my thoughts to rest.

I woke up the next morning to the most beautiful sunrise, with Saudi Arabia in the distance and thought, this is a magical place. I wanted to soak it all in. I was still unable to communicate with Oron. I spoke to Marla and asked to be alone during my time there. When I wasn't alone, I talked to other guests in the campground. This place was so healing, and I felt a spiritual connection, a sense of ease, even amongst the discord I felt. Every day, I went for a swim in the ocean and lay in the water, looking up at the sky, praying to God for answers. I sought my purpose in life and to get rid of the pit in my stomach, and ease my heavy heart. It was then, when I was lost and floating in a foreign sea, that I found my voice with God. "Why am I here? What should I do? What am I doing here" After a few days of talking to God, something shifted for me; I began to feel lighter, guided so clearly that these feelings almost felt tangible. Prayer became my foundation for everything. I was safe and trusted that I was being guided.

I decided to make amends with Oron by apologizing to him for how I had been relating to him, although it felt awkward initially, in that moment it was the only way I thought things could get better. His response was arrogant and extremely unpleasant. "It's about time"

155

he said, exasperated, along with a few choice names I shall not mention. I chose to accept his response because I didn't see the point in arguing, when I was leaving in a few days to go home.

Oron decided we would "celebrate" by having dinner at another campground close by.

About twenty minutes into our drive, Oron looked at Marla and said, "I think we passed the place." They laughed and kept driving. Then he would turn to her and say, "Tell me to turn around." They laughed and continued driving.

We continued driving a little longer and on the opposite side of this two lane road surrounded by mountains was a bus which appeared to be abandoned. As we approached the front of the bus, a man suddenly jumped out in front of us. Oron couldn't swerve in time, and the man's body hit the hood of the car windshield, and proceeded to roll over the roof. The impact was so intense, the man broke through the rear window shield, and I felt his hand hit my neck.

Next thing we knew, twenty to twenty-five Egyptians who had been sitting in the shade behind the bus came running out, screaming in Arabic in response to this tragic scene. The man lay on the roof of our car with his head split open, while we desperately tried to prolong his life by pouring water on him. We asked drivers to help us, but no one stopped. It took an hour for someone to finally stop and rush him to the hospital. Sadly, the efforts were not timely enough, and the man eventually died. We were taken to the border police station. All I could say was, "I don't care what happens between today and tomorrow, as long as I'm on a plane back home on Saturday." I prayed once again and felt I was safe and trusted, that I was being guided.

We spent several hours at the police station, answering officer's questions and providing free entertainment for the locals. After the majority of our questioning was done, day turned to night, and Marla returned to our campsite to gather our belongings. An hour or so later, Oron said to me, "You don't have to stay here. Why don't you get in a cab and go meet Marla?" I couldn't see a thing as I stepped into the pitch-black night. I managed to make out a cab and asked the driver if he would take me to our campgrounds. As we drove into nothingness, I thought to myself, "This man can take me away and no one would find me." And then I felt that familiar presence once again. Silence and Trust. I was being guided. I was safe.

We arrived at the campground, where I was met with a screaming Marla, angry with me for leaving Oron alone at the police station, Marla was oblivious of how the whole situation had impacted me. We rushed back to the police station to find Oron still sitting there, waiting for us, it had been several more hours during this second visit of mine to the station, and I reminded Marla that we didn't need to stay there.

"Oron will need to follow the protocol, but we can leave," I said. She refused to see my point of view, so around midnight, I made the decision to walk across the border alone.

As I walked to the border alone in the dark, I could feel God's hands on my shoulder, and was reminded again that I was far from alone. I felt God's presence and knew that I would be taken care of. My plan was to spend the night in a hotel and then get a ride to Tel Aviv. As I was filling out the paperwork at the border customs, I was approached by a young man asking if he could use my pen. To my good fortune, I found out this man was also traveling to Tel Aviv, so I asked if there was room for one more person in his car (something I had never done and most certainly never felt safe enough to do in the U.S.) He said yes. We jumped in the taxi, traveled several hours overnight, and thankfully I made it back to my apartment in time for my flight back home.

On my return flight, I began to reflect on the past couple of weeks. I thought back to the times of anger and peace, and realized that the purpose of my trip was to confront these crossroads. Journaling became my way of expressing all that had transpired, and then, suddenly a wave of calmness came over me, but this time it was different. Unlike the days I had spent floating in the ocean searching for answers, only to have those feelings of peace slowly fade away, this calmness came from within. I knew that it was time for me to choose. Do I go down the path of anger in hopes of a reconciliation with my sister, or do I choose peace, and accept the loss of this relationship in my life? Do I take this new inner peace and walk away from this relationship? I chose walking away from the relationship, and although it was the most difficult experience of my life, I had never felt so liberated and free. I learned that my Intuition is powerful, and it guided me the down most difficult path and now I understand that it's in the difficult moments that I get to grow, expand and become the woman I envisioned.

This trip changed everything for me, or rather, I changed everything about how I relate to myself. I found my power by choosing the path of love, and in turn, all the relationships in my life that did not reflect this, faded away. I was clear in my choice that our relationship did not serve my highest good. As I walked up my front steps to my home, I noticed the pain I felt in my stomach at the beginning of the trip had become a distant memory. I began to feel a wholeness reside in its absence. I realized this trip wasn't about reconnecting with my sister, and the answer was there all the time. I knew it the second I stepped into Oron's car when I arrived. This trip wasn't about Marla or Oron. It was my journey to Self-Discovery and Self-Love.

I had reconnected to Self through the crossroads, and I'm never going back.

Tools that work and feel natural:

1) Prayer: Everyone prays differently. How I move into prayer is by asking for guidance, and having an authentic conversation with my higher power. I have a conversation and listen for the answers without doubt or fear.

2) Intuition: Be Still and the answer is always there. Listen as you ask yourself a question. Feel the sensation or thoughts that are coming to you.

3) Journaling: Write what comes to you. Your thoughts and experience are always important to express in writing. This integrates for most people the understanding of clarity.

Michelle Mor

A Woman's Heart

"You just seemed like the lady next door,
so down to earth, easy to relate to,
I found myself listening to you more and more
during the podcast series!"
~ Margaretta from my online community – Australia

I'm just a country girl living in Ireland, down to earth, easy to relate to. Today I'm living a deeply fulfilling life of Inner Peace, Love and Happiness!

Being a very determined, committed person, with a lot of grit, I've worked hard to achieve this way of being. But it wasn't always like this. What I love about my life is the natural wisdom that I draw on when conversing with other people. I love seeing the expression in their eyes as aha's begin to show up for them through my conversations. What I find amazing about my life right now is the calming, soothing disposition I have and the gift of healing that comes through my talents in music and voice. People have spoken about my aura – golden in color – and also the healing light-energy that I portray when playing the harp.

WE ALL HAVE A STORY

Mine began when I was 16 years of age. I was forced to leave school due to a long-term illness. I was diagnosed with an anxiety disorder called epilepsy and the stress of school exams activated the symptoms. I was always collapsing and bruising my body as I fell to the ground with my full body weight. My facial expression changed during the blackouts. My speech would become slurred. People around me became frightened and shied away from me. I was very much alone, and my experience was one of shame, fear, unworthiness. I felt very ugly, as a person who wondered what others were thinking and saying about me. My thoughts were full of low self-worth and low self-esteem.

By the end of this chapter, you will discover 3 strategies to overcome inner emotional pain, anxiety disorders, and disempowerment. You will see how to achieve breakthroughs to completely love yourself and establish emotional peace leading to a deeply fulfilling life!

I didn't know then what I know now, but this was the root cause of my core problem of unhappiness and searching within, which showed up as emotional challenges, anxieties, struggles, and insecurities.

I used to feel very unhappy, full of inner loss and sensing – something I was to find out later through an awakening – that I was on a deep soul search. The feeling of this soul search was so horrendous:

- I was searching for something but didn't know what I was searching for!

- I would feel incomplete, lacking in something, really discontent – I was weak and disempowered!

WORKSHEET QUESTIONS

1. What is your BIGGEST desire, the one that lives deep down inside your own secret place within, that you tell nobody about?

   _____

   _____

2. What type of lifestyle do you want to live and WHY do you want this?

   _____

   _____

3. What is the GAP between where you are now and where you want to be?

   _____

   _____

4. What are you DETERMINED to work through and transform today to fulfill your deepest desires?

_____

_____

SHIFTING UP GEARS

I have been an Award Winning Celtic Harpist for over 40 years; I founded a school of music called the Armagh Harpers' Association, which teaches and promotes the instrument with weekly classes, workshops, events, and concerts. One of my main projects was organizing a harp music festival in 1996 to help raise awareness, during a time when Irish-harping was a dying culture in Ireland. I had a strong passion to become part of a movement to help restore the harp and its music, saving it for posterity. Highly dedicated students came to learn from me – not only the music but also the art form of emotionally connecting with the music on a soul level. Today I also mentor as a Personal Development Coach. I use some of those same modalities to assist people in finding emotional healing, inner peace, joy and happiness in life.

When I first started mentoring and teaching, I had no idea, no inkling, where it would lead. Looking back over the last 40 years of my life, I remember my first client reached out to me after I was awarded the All-Ireland Fleadh Cheoil Prize. I had just won the senior harp competition and achieving that award was one of my power moments. It felt A-MA-ZING!

Throughout my life, I have felt a strong pull towards my goals and visions. I had gone through a spiritual awakening in 2003 and gained emotional fulfillment through the work I do guiding thousands of women to find inner peace, healing, joy, and happiness.

I didn't know at 18 that I was starting out on a journey that would lead to my life's legacy as coach and healer who would serve the people who came across my path. My inspiration has come through the people I hang out with, both offline and online and the books I read. I highly recommend the audiobook "The War of Art," by Steven Pressfield and "The Artist's Way," by Julia Cameron for learning how to break through limiting beliefs as a creative individual.

A MOMENT THAT CHANGED MY LIFE FOREVER

In 2003 I went on a pilgrimage to Medjugorje, a town in Bosnia and Herzegovina and I had the most profound spiritual experience there.

I was blessed with an apparition, a vision which was breathtaking! Among the many gifts I have been given since are the gifts of inner peace and healing – this is what I'm here to do, and I want to help people tap into the inner peace I have discovered.

I have been taught by my coaches and mentors the tools and strategies that I teach today. To these tools, I would like to share with you the tools to reach that inner peace I was blessed to have experienced.

MY STORY GOES LIKE THIS

During that time, I was experiencing deep loss and pain: my marriage was ending, my security was shattered, my life was completely shaken up and I felt I was dying inside. Then one night, as I was alone in my bed, I experienced an awful sensation. I could hear what sounded like paper bags being crunched up between someone's hands. I felt a presence in the bedroom. I felt I was being gripped by a dark force.

As I reached for rosary beads from under my pillow, I was being held back from reciting the rosary. Held back as in unable to speak. I remember wrapping the rosary beads around my fingers, imploring intervention from above but feeling this "held-back" experience again. At that moment, I felt very frightened. My eyes closed tight in EXTREME FEAR and this fear created paralysis.

Then I slowly opened my eyes and there was the most beautiful apparition of a silhouette vision, vivid in color, standing the full length of the bedroom door. But because I was shocked, I closed my eyes very quickly. When I reopened them, the image was gone. I hoped that the image would reappear, but nothing.

The vision only gave me that one chance to see her! I had mixed feelings and remained skeptical for years. Did this really happen? Did I imagine it?

LOOKING BACK IN HINDSIGHT

I had reached out for protection, help, and intervention against the dark force and I received a religious/spiritual experience. Then this week I was sharing the experience with one of my coaching clients and that's when I realized some major Aha's. Here are my realizations:

- The Rosary beads represented – surrendering to a higher power.

- The noisy paper bags and the paralysis – being gripped by a dark force.

- Turning for help – that's protection.

- And the Vision – a heightened spiritual awareness and connection.

I HAVE BEEN GIVEN GIFTS

I have been given special gifts of inner peace, wisdom, enduring spiritual grace and joy to share with the world. I know this is why my work is so profoundly important.

In 2014 I signed up with a business coach to learn to expand deeper into my niche. I learned personal development and spiritual development in this program which uncovered parts of my shadow that I had to face along my journey. These were my deepest fears, my resistance to change, my resistance to turning around and looking with honesty at my true self. I worked diligently through my deep-set beliefs and patterns and, as I allowed myself to expand and grow, I become able to hold more.

What I've realized about myself is that through my surrendering and forgiveness, I have received many gifts to share with the world to make the world a better place. These gifts are empathy, aestheticism, deep wisdom, inner guidance, kindness, knowledge, tools, music, healing, composing and creating, connection and FREEDOM!

I've expanded my growth and will always continue to learn from others. My passion is all about helping others through their emotional pain-points to rise up to brilliance and have a better quality of life. I have a great community of coaches and mentors today!

Patricia Daly

Be Your Best Advocate

"Be your body's best advocate so that you can make informed
decisions about your emotional and physical health.
If you don't take the initiative and care for yourself,
you can't expect anyone else to, either."
~ Bonnie Gayle

I have not felt the way I do today about my physical and mental health for most of my life. I'm sharing my story and I know it may be heavy for many. However, I want you to know that no matter what you go through in life, you can overcome it and get to the other side.

When I was growing up, I never really thought about health, wellness, or that I needed to take care of myself. My parents would take me to the doctor for checkups, but other than that, I did nothing to make sure I was healthy, inside or out. In fact, the only time I ever really thought about my health was when I got sick.

Basically, I had a very passive approach to taking care of myself. In fact, I did a lot of things that ended up breaking down my body prematurely, resulting in health issues later in life.

At the age of 16 I was violently raped and almost choked to death on the rapist's penis. He stopped because I was turning blue. I was so shocked because this was someone I knew from school. What was even more painful was that I had to keep this a secret for two reasons. First, my parents would have kept me from going out with friends and I already had the earliest curfew of anyone I knew. There was also another student who was raped two months earlier, and when the story got out, everyone blamed her. She ended up leaving school because the gossip got so bad. I was afraid the same thing would happen to me if people found out, so I suffered in silence.

At the time, I was a runner and ended up getting injured five times in a year. I was told I had to stop running. Running was my only escape after the rape. The loss of my ability to run, along with the horrifying nightmares that I experienced after the rape, crushed my self-esteem so much that I ended up eating myself into a lethargy over the next year.

I didn't even realize what I was doing to myself until one of my coaches took me aside and told me that he was worried about me. What he noticed was that I was miserable most of the time and had gained a lot of weight. Little did he know that the conversation with him got my attention more then he knew and set me off on a tailspin.

When I got home, I weighed myself and was in shock at the scale. I had to check it three times because I couldn't believe the number. I had gained 60 pounds in a little under a year. I ran into my room, cried for hours, and was inconsolable. How did I get so big without even realizing it? I was always an athlete and I experienced a healthy growth spurt at an early age, so I was always taller and bigger than everyone else. But I wasn't heavy, especially after I started running.

Yes, I compared my body to other girls, but I was always taller, so it seemed natural that I weighed more too. Not this time. I had been using food to numb out as I grieved the loss of running and the rape. I was officially fat and emotionally distraught. Not a good combination.

I knew I had to lose the weight or I would continue to be miserable. So, I did what most people do – I went on diet after diet hoping to find the magical fix for me. This only made matters worse and I became really frustrated. It was a vicious cycle of restricting, and then bingeing when I couldn't take it anymore. It became so painful that I turned to something that almost killed me at the age of 28, bulimia. Bulimia is a process of binging (overeating) and purging (deliberate vomiting) which is designed to control your weight.

I was introduced to bulimia by a friend who was also an athlete. At first, I thought, "I could never do that," but in no time, I was bingeing and then purging everything I ate. I was so obsessed with being thin again that I was throwing up 20 times a day and that went on for thirteen years

Believe it or not, I was fully functional during this process. I was in school full time until I graduated, getting straight A's, and I worked part time until I finished school. After I graduated, I worked full time without anyone knowing of my disease, until the last year or two when my mom finally figured it out. She forced me to go to therapy but that didn't work because I wasn't ready. I needed to want help and I didn't until a year or two later. That is when my healing began.

Once I started doing the inner work to deal with my screwed-up thinking, I stopped the bingeing and purging. What I didn't know at the time was that I had already done a lot of damage to my body. I had problems with digestion, elimination, and almost ended up poisoning myself because my body wasn't processing food properly. I became toxic because I was only able to eliminate once every eleven days or so. My body was retaliating from years of abuse and was gaining a lot of weight.

I knew nothing about health, nutrition, or what was good or bad for my body until my 30s when I partnered with a naturalist who taught me about food and nutrition. This newfound knowledge started me on a new path of eating. I eliminated bread, pasta, and anything made of wheat.

As I learned more, my eating became more refined and by the age of 41 I was eating mostly organic and reading labels. I had eliminated processed and canned foods and dairy. I also cut way back on anything that had sugar and I finally started feeling better. That year I unexpectedly started peri-menopause which brought its own challenges. My body began changing again but this time it was hormone induced – hot flashes, night sweats, brain fog, and vaginal atrophy. I felt like I was falling apart all over again.

I chose to heal my challenges holistically with alternative methods to western medicine. This turned out to be a good thing because years later, my mom developed breast cancer which metastasized to her liver and ended up killing her. Our family had no history of female cancer, but my mom had been on a particular type of hormone replacement therapy for years that ended up being pulled off the market because so many women who took it got cancer. I am so grateful I chose to heal myself without taking hormones.

When it comes to taking care of your body, you must be your body's best advocate because the choices you make control your health and well-being. It may not sound like a big deal, but it is. When you're walking around in pain, whether it's physical or emotional, it affects everything you say and do in life. It also affects people around you; family, friends, coworkers, and more.

You may be wondering what it means to be your body's best advocate and what that really looks like. It is a practice, and knowledge is power. The more aware you are and the more you feel "into" your body, the easier it is to see what works for you and what doesn't. I'm talking about things you can control in your life, such as food, body products, cleaning products, household products, drinking water and your lifestyle.

Food is a big contributor because there are so many things being done to food today that most things we think of as food are not. They are chemicals made to look like food that have little or no nutritional value. Your body doesn't recognize these chemical compounds as food, so it creates inflammation to protect itself. Inflammation was meant to be temporary, not chronic. If you are eating these so-called foods regularly, you end up with chronic inflammation, the root cause of all disease.

Fast forward to my 50s. Even though I was eating the same, I gained weight for the first time in years. Within two years, I had gained 20 pounds and this time it wasn't because I was eating a lot of junk. I knew all the right things to eat, so that wasn't the issue. I was also exercising, walking an hour a day every morning. What I didn't know was that I had chronic inflammation that was keeping me from getting rid of this excess weight.

After a lot of research, I changed my eating once again to an anti-inflammatory diet and quickly eliminated the menopause weight. I have effortlessly kept it off ever since. I do exercise, but not excessively and I eat food that I love. Once I knew the cause of my weight gain, I was able to remedy the situation and correct the problem. By doing the research and acting on the findings, I was my body's best advocate.

The products you use on and in your body, may be wreaking havoc and causing disease. Parabens can cause female cancers, and Propylene Glycol is the main ingredient in antifreeze. These two ingredients are in many body products and cosmetics. Most of you aren't aware of the thousands of toxic chemicals your skin absorbs that go straight into your bloodstream. They are harmful and should never have been allowed in these products. There is no regulation, so you must advocate for yourself or you could be harming yourself and not even know it.

Products in your environment make a big difference in your health. Everything from cleaning products, toilet paper, plastic, cans, storage containers, scented air fresheners, Kleenex, and more. If they are made and infused with toxic chemicals, you are breathing and wearing these chemicals, which are being absorbed into your body.

If you're wondering what you can do, awareness is the first step. If you don't know there's a problem, you can't remedy it.

When it comes to food, eat an anti-inflammatory diet. Not only do you want to make sure you're eating anti-inflammatory food, they should also be organic, hormone- and antibiotic-free.

Conventionally grown produce is loaded with chemicals your body doesn't recognize as food. Avoid food that comes in BPA-lined cans or plastic if possible because they leach hormone mimickers, creating inflammation. Read food labels, and if you don't know what something is, look it up. Don't eat chemicals, flavorings, refined foods, or artificial sweeteners.

When it comes to body products, buy organic. Dr. Bronner's makes some great body products you can dilute in water. They are cost efficient and feel good. Use toilet paper that is eco-friendly and chemical free. Take care of your precious parts. Read labels and don't use products that contain chemicals.

The same goes for anything in your environment, including your furniture. Take preventative measures and you will be surprised at how much better you feel. I have been able to live medication-free in a highly stressful environment by making some simple changes.

I'm not suggesting you go off medication but if you start to eliminate the causes of the symptoms you are experiencing, you may find that you don't need it. By being your body's best advocate and having awareness, you can make educated decisions for yourself that could allow you to live a greater quality of life.

Awareness is the first step to being your body's best advocate. Educating yourself and taking action on what you know is key. Choose to be your body's best advocate and don't put your health and well-being into someone else's hands because they may not have your best interests at heart. To start looking and feeling your best, enjoy these amazing tips of organic and clean-living solutions!

Bonnie Gayle

Pandemic In Our Country: Where psychological and gut health intersect, and how the healing begins.

"Let food be thy medicine and medicine be thy food"
~ Hippocrates

Pick up any newspaper, magazine, or turn on the television and there is story after story of shootings, hostages, self-inflicted wounds, deaths and more. How close does it have to hit home before we start connecting the dots?

My heart broke when I heard the devastating news about the husband of my daughter's best friend. A young man, who is a son, husband and father of two beautiful children, found himself in a psych ward, trying to make sense of all the chaos in his family's life.

If you've had close contact with someone who suffers from depression, anxiety, or any other physiological disorder, you know it's really like a crap shoot. From moment to moment, life can and does change. Typically, the go-to answer is prescription medicine and, in some cases, talk therapy. The problem is these treatments mask the symptoms and don't delve into the underlying issues.

You might be wondering how our brain and our gut (digestive system) might be related, and how they work synergistically together. Our gut contains approximately 3.5 pounds of essential bacteria and over 100 trillion cells for producing products that our brain and organs need. I've learned that an ideal ratio is about 85% good bacteria to about 15% bad bacteria. That will give you healthy gut flora. While more research needs to be done to determine which strains of bacteria are most beneficial for brain health, lactobacillus, found in yogurt and fermented foods, like Kimchi, raw sauerkraut, kefir, kombucha and bifidobacterial can produce tryptophan which regulates appetite, sexual desire, our mood as well as other tasks in the body. Both lactobacillus and tryptophan have been shown to help with mental health. The overuse of antibiotics is can damage our mental health, by wiping out gut flora.

In one study, healthy rats were given probiotics to wipe out all bacteria in their gut system. Microbiome was taken from depressed patients and inserted into the gut system of the mice and they too became depressed and developed a pro-inflammatory system.

"Wherever there is mental distress, there is digestive distress," according to Dr. Leslie Korn, Nutrition Essentials for Mental Health: A Complete Guide to the Food-Mood Connection. Dr. Korn is an integrative medicine and mental health expert, trained at the Harvard School of Public Health. She states "The brain is not always the cause of mental illness." More specifically, she says, "research shows that low levels of inflammatory process in the body underlie depression, anxiety" and other mental and cognitive disorders. At the same time, healthy bacteria "regulate inflammatory process in the body."

When someone has a compromised gut, often referred to as "leaky gut," the intestinal walls allow food particles into the bloodstream. That leads to out-of-control inflammation. Inflammation is the body's natural response to trauma. With a cut, homeostasis begins after the wound is inflicted – the blood vessels constrict and seal themselves off as the platelets create substances that form a clot and halt bleeding. Once homeostasis is achieved, the blood vessels dilate, letting nutrients, white blood cells, antibodies, enzymes and other beneficial elements into the affected area. They promote good wound healing and stave off infection. This is when someone experiences the first physical effects of inflammation – swelling, pain, heat and redness.

How do you know if you have a distressed and out-of-balance digestive system?

    1)   Digestive Issues

Gas

Bloating

Irritable Bowel Syndrome (IBS)

Irritable Bowel Disease (Crohn's and Ulcerative

Colitis)

Constipation

Diarrhea

If you find these issues happen on a regular basis, your doctor might prescribe medications or antacids. They mask the issue, but don't uncover root cause.

2)   Deficiencies of Vitamins and Minerals

When there is an unhealthy gut environment, the body has a hard time utilizing the vitamins it is receiving from food. To find out if you are deficient, ask your doctor to test your levels, especially Vitamin B, Vitamin D, Vitamin K, and Magnesium.

3)   Mental Health Issues

Scientists have known for the past several decades that there is direct communication between the brain and the gastrointestinal (GI) tract. Statistics show that 90% of the serotonin produced in the body is found in the gut. Serotonin is a neurotransmitter responsible for regulating appetite, mood, sleep, and relaxation.

Gut bacteria influence the communication between the brain and the gut. When the gut is full of healthy bacteria, it can regulate mood and positive feelings. Low levels of GABA (gamma-Aminobutyric acid), a neurotransmitter, may also be linked to anxiety, more mood disorders, epilepsy and chronic pain.

As Canadian neuroscientist Jane Foster states, "The cross talk between the gut biome and the brain is continual. That's the important take-home message. These are not two separate systems; they are two parts of a single system."

4)   Chronic Stress

Most of us know that heightened levels of stress cause us to go into fight or flight mode, which affects the blood flow to the gut. This explains why we might experience some digestive disorders after a round of high stress.

Consistent and long-term stress erodes the good guys in our bacterial colony. Remember I mentioned that we like the balance to be about 85% good to 15% bad bacteria? If we upset this ecosystem, it starts to affect how we feel, look, and act.

5)   Skin Disorders

A primary role of the gut is to absorb the nutrients from food that your body needs for healthy functioning, growth, and repair. When the body doesn't receive enough nutrients, it begins to prioritize which organs will get the few nutrients that are available. Your skin, nails and hair are generally the first places you will see changes. This happens because the body will protect vital organs first, such as the brain, heart, and liver.

Because your skin is the largest organ, it makes sense that the appearance of the skin would be in direct correlation to what's going on inside your body, especially your gut health. Acne, eczema, psoriasis, dry skin, rosacea and redness of the face are skin conditions which all have the same root cause – gut health.

6)   Autoimmune Disease

I mentioned previously that we need to keep a nice healthy balance of good bacteria (85%) to bad (15%)

because our gut health accounts for about 80% of our immune system. When that balance gets disrupted, the good bacteria will die off and the bad ones start to take over. Antibiotics play a big role, throwing you off balance. The good bacteria get killed off or greatly reduced and the bad bacteria takes over and grows out of control. This includes yeast (Candida overgrowth) and Small Intestinal Bacteria Overgrowth (SIBO).

Diet plays a huge role in this response as well. If you are eating a typical diet that is high in refined carbs, alcohol and sugar, you are feeding the SIBO and Candida, which in turn lets them take control. That's called dysbiosis. I mentioned antibiotics as a culprit, but we can't leave out birth control pills, acid blockers and steroids. These treatments can and do cause more dysbiosis, which ultimately suppresses your immune system, which then leads to further infections and disease, which leads to more prescriptions. And the hamster wheel continues.

Eventually this is where leaky gut, as mentioned above, comes into play. Your immune system sees the food particles and toxins as foreign invaders, sounds the alarm and starts attacking them, which creates inflammation. Your body sees many of these food particles as the enemy because they look like our own body's cells. So now it has crossed signals and starts attacking its own tissues. That leads to autoimmunity, also called molecular mimicry, which leads to autoimmune disease.

Some types of autoimmune disease are:

Addison's disease
Celiac disease
Graves' disease
Hashimoto
Inflammatory bowel disease
Multiple sclerosis
Rheumatoid arthritis
Lupus
And many others.

As you can see, if our foundation (gut health) isn't strong, neither are we. For many, this starts before birth. There is evidence of weakened immunity in the fetal tissues when a mother has taken antibiotics during the pregnancy. The health of the mother plays a big role in the health of her unborn child and their gut microbiome. If the child is born vaginally, they swallow a good dose of good bacteria upon birth and again through breast milk. If a baby is delivered by C-section, they don't receive these bacteria. If they are fed formula, they also miss out on beneficial antibodies to help boost their immune system.

At this point, it may seem hopeless if you, or someone you know, is afflicted with one or more of these issues. I'm here to say there is hope, health, and healing for all. This fact is often overlooked as we scramble to find relief from our afflictions. Rather than permanently avoiding gluten, dairy, grains, or any other allergens that cause you grief, let's look at the healing process. Let's become tolerant because avoidance doesn't help us heal.

A functional medicine approach is a straight-forward one.

    a.   Remove

    b.   Replace

    c.   Reinoculate

    d.   Repair

At the beginning, you remove all known allergens, such as gluten, dairy, corn, soy, grains, alcohol, drugs, caffeine, and sugar. They are most often the source of irritants and inflammation. Good food allergen testing, and stool samples are necessary to determine what, if any, infections are present and what the levels of good to bad bacteria are. Parasites are a very real issue for many, and it may be necessary to deal with these, along with anti-fungal meds or supplements. This creates an ideal environment for healing.

The second phase is to start adding back the good stuff by replacing hydrochloric acid, bile, and enzymes for digestion and uptake of vital nutrients.

The third phase is to start reinoculating the gut with good bacteria. It is recommended that anywhere from 80-100 billion units a day of a good pharmaceutical grade probiotics be taken. Don't forget about prebiotics as well, either in supplement form or by eating higher fiber foods.

The fourth phase, in my opinion, is the most important: healing and repairing the gut lining. My favorite is to use bone broth, which is loaded with collagen (rich in amino acids) and anti-inflammatory ingredients to quiet down and sooth the gut. A good collagen supplement can also be taken, as well as L-glutamine, high quality omega-3 fish oils, and colostrums.

Our society likes instant gratification. I'm not saying that these steps are speedy. I believe you will see marked improvements along the way, enough to keep you motivated and on the path to hope, health and healing. I am a firm believer that you were given a fine-tuned body, or temple, as I like to call it. Your body knows how to heal itself. You just need to supply the right tools, have the desire to make the necessary changes and know this is a lifelong journey.

I want to give you a high five for devouring what you've read, taking it to heart, and then taking action that will literally change your life or a loved one's life. The next step is get involved with a good functional medicine doctor. I also recommend a good coaching program to keep you on track and accountable to yourself and the decisions you've decided are best for you.

The final step: spread the word. As Dr. Weston A. Price once stated, "You teach, you teach, you teach." Start with yourself, family members, and friends. We each have a powerful network and if we teach each other and make the changes necessary, we can change the world around us, mentally and physically.

Kellie Valenti

Love Revolution

To Recovery With Love

"It's difficult to believe in yourself because the idea of self is an artificial construction.
You are, in fact, part of the glorious oneness of the universe.
Everything beautiful in the world is within you."
~ Russell Brand

Recovery gets a bad rap. The connotation comes off as something negative, difficult, and usually shameful. But look at the word: "Re-cov-er-y. Noun. A return to a normal state of health, mind or strength."

In this crazy, mixed-up world, who doesn't want and aspire to that state of being? I know one thing. Recovery has changed my life. Recovery has created a life for me that I could never have imagined, and it just keeps getting better. Of course, I didn't always know this.

The first time I went into a recovery program it was mandated. I went in kicking and screaming (internally) with an attitude of *"just get through this – I am different from everyone else. I don't really need this. Look how messed up they are* (pointing fingers)." Because I was always able to present myself as a good girl, a nice person and a refined woman, I got a pass. I was in an outpatient treatment program.

The treatment program stuck for a while. But of course, I slowly but surely slipped into past behavior. A little here, a sneak of it there. And of course, my husband at the time was a willing participant – unless it was more beneficial for him to point fingers and let me know what a horribly awful person I was for no longer being the perfect wife he fantasized about. And God knows I was never that.

If you have an addiction, you know. The larger your addiction looms, the more out of control you become, the louder that voice in your head screams, "What is wrong with you?" "What a loser you are." "Why can't, why won't you stop?" "What's it going to take?"

In my case what it would take was blacking out. Waking up after a weekend of fun and wine tasting. A glass by my bed. A bottle of wine in the closet. And my daughter opening the door, looking at me with such disappointment and quiet desperation, then closing the door and leaving. My heart broke in two and I surrendered.

> *"A deep sense of love and belonging is*
> *an irreducible need of all people.*
> *We are biologically, cognitively, physically,*
> *and spiritually wired to love, to be loved,*
> *and to belong. When those needs are not met,*
> *we don't function as we were meant to.*
> *We break. We fall apart. We numb. We ache.*

Love Revolution

We hurt others. We get sick. "
~ Brené Brown

Off to detox I went. This time with a purpose. A realization that I was going to lose the one person in my life that meant everything if I didn't get sober. To say it was difficult was an understatement. The three days in detox are safe. It's like being in a cocoon, away from the world and monitored, with classes and meetings, surrounded by people with similar problems, and no access to the things and people that trigger you.

Re-entering the world sober is the hard part. Knowing the changes that need to be made (and I had so many) was overwhelming. In my case I was married to an addict and our entire social world revolved around alcohol and drugs. My marriage was no longer loving, it was abusive and frightening. Giving up alcohol with its delightful, numbing properties was scary in this situation. I remember coming home from a recovery meeting and there was a roaring party going on. It was a birthday celebration for my husband, so I had to smile and try to engage like it was all OK.

You may have a similar situation. It isn't easy to begin extricating yourself from your problem.

The next few years had their ups and downs. The first year of sobriety was incredibly difficult. There was a lot of white knuckling (I don't recommend this) and just getting through the days. But I was regaining a better sense of myself slowly. Enough so that when my husband came home after a day of drinking, becoming more and more belligerent and aggressive, I took our daughter and fled to safety. I realized I could no longer subject either of us to this kind of treatment.

She and I moved to a new home, and I decided then and there that I would never do things that I did not want to do. I wanted to live life on my terms. I took an out-of-town class where I met new friends. This was a key to my new sober life. Creating relationships that were healthy. I was able to rearrange my livelihood into a business I absolutely loved doing. It fed my creative spirit which had taken a back seat to my addiction and left such a void. I remember buying a car – one that suited me perfectly, and how empowering that was.

The next big leap was getting involved in a network marketing company with a friend. I met a new group of women I admire to this day. I was exposed to the most incredible trainings and teachers. I immersed myself with the coaches in the self-help world I didn't even know existed. I traveled and explored.

This became my version of AA (remember, it doesn't matter where it comes from for you). As the products were in health, I became a product of the product (as I was taught). As I became slimmer and more vibrant, people started asking me what I was doing. They asked me for my help. As I so desperately needed to find my self-worth and value, this was a new beginning.

In a few years, I made another big move to a new city, went back to school to pursue Health Coaching, and my current career and livelihood was born. After fifteen years into my recovery, I can only say that I could not have possibly known how things would end up. Each year gets better as I continue to grow in my body, mind and spirit.

Self-care is not an option. It is a requirement. Make sure to create loving rituals for yourself, like having beautiful flowers, massages, and spa experiences, even if they are at home. Use essential oils for spirit and health, eat whole nutritious food, leave sugar and processed foods behind. Create good sleep habits.

Don't allow yourself to get "hangry" (angry and hungry = hangry), it causes bad choices. Make sure you move your body. In fact, as I write this, I am immersed in Yoga Teacher Training. Yoga is adding to my spiritual health, which is the one piece of life I still felt was lacking.

I'm sure you might have questions. I know I did. I took tests trying to prove I didn't have a problem (didn't work very well).

I have created a process inspired by the 7 stages of grief. Letting go of your addiction is a release akin to a death of sorts. It will leave a void that you will want to fill, as you've been filling that empty void with every distraction and substance you can think of.

PROCESS

1) Confusion:

   Who am I? Am I an addict? (I started questioning this early in life as so many of my family members were alcoholics).

2) Possibility:

   It could be possible. *(Uh oh. Really?)*

3) Probability:

   I probably am. *(Oh, Shit!)*

4) Acceptance:

   This is who I am. (Here is the pivot. This is where change comes from.) Now I need to deal with it. Action.

5) Take Pride:

   Embrace myself. (This is where self-care becomes monumental)

6) Integration to Life:

   Create meaningful relationships, learn to live on your own terms, let go of relationships that no longer serve you.

There are so many paths to recover from your addiction. There is no one size fits all. We need to honor every path and the journey it takes to get there. I suggest you approach recovery with love. A good recovery program (of which the 12 steps is one) is designed to break the mental patterns that keep us stuck. We need to connect to new ways to perceive things, connect to new relationships that are healthy, and then re-enter "life."

This is the age of addiction. We are all recovering from something. Smoking, alcohol, drugs, sex, overeating, bulimia, gambling, bad relationships, overspending, and we can't even take our eyes away from our constant screen time. At some point we lost our way. Addiction replaces the uncomfortable feelings we have within ourselves. Addicts are masters at avoidance. We learn to skirt around and suppress our own feelings.

Self-compassion is one of the best recovery tools I know of. It decreases the body's cortisol levels and promotes the production and release of oxytocin, a neurological chemical that reduces cravings. This is not the time to isolate. Find people that will support you in your journey in a healthy, loving way. We crave connection. Recovery is a journey to wholeness. Mind, body and spirit.

We do not need to hit rock bottom. At any point, we can realize that our addiction is a disruption to our normal behaviors, morality and well-being. We can decide to change. We can focus on our strengths instead of our weaknesses. Learn from our past and make peace with our present. It takes time. Be patient. Acknowledge your mistakes, and then let them go. Write them down and create a ritual around burning each one as you release them. Remember, you are exactly where you need to be right now – there is no need to race through life. Give yourself some slack, allowing yourself the time and permission to move on to better things. I know you will find new aspects of yourself that will delight you.

Recover the person you were meant to be. It takes courage, strength, commitment and faith. Recovery from anything is the most courageous thing a person can do. Focusing on Self-growth is a process that will serve you in every aspect of your life. Speak to yourself as though you are your dearest friend. Look in the mirror and give yourself a loving affirmation. Do this every day.

Find a loving acceptance of self, a mindful nurturing of your physical body, and a commitment to purposeful living. You will look back and wonder why it took you so long to take the step into recovery. This is what I wish for you.

Be Love.

Sharon Otness

Comedy, Tragedy, And Loving Who You Are

"Comedy is acting out optimism."
~ Robin Williams

It has been said that there's a thin line between comedy and tragedy. If you have ever looked back on your teenage years, you know that's true. Not being asked to the prom was most definitely a tragedy (what, just me?), but time has softened that blow considerably.

Sometimes though, everything can seem tragic and it can overtake our lives. I know it did mine, inevitably resulting in a diagnosis of depression. It's a label I wore for around 20 years. It made sense. I was tired all the time and I didn't really like anything, so at least I could wear that badge of honor proudly to explain why I wasn't getting anywhere in life.

I take it back – I got somewhere, just nowhere that I wanted to be. I graduated with a business degree with honors, then I got an MBA by 23 for good measure. I didn't like any of it, so to top it off I got a government job. I don't need to say any more about that.

I accomplished a fair bit in terms of what the average person might think of as life goals, but I hated all of it. I found business just soulless, and the bureaucracy of government absolutely soul-crushing. I needed an outlet of some kind or else I would go mad.

I tried to learn guitar at least three times in two decades. I was a musician by training, but for some reason, I just couldn't master it – maybe bleeding fingers and calluses turned me off. Who knows?

On a whim, I had an idea for a children's book. I have no idea why or where it came from. So, one day, after another boring day at my job, I sat down with a glass of wine on my balcony and jotted down a story in 45 minutes. I eventually self-published that book.

I'm not saying whether wine was critical to this or not.

But all the while, I was still searching for something that felt like "me." I said I wanted to be a writer, but I barely wrote. Yeah, that's kind of a problem. I had trouble motivating myself to do anything, really.

It would seem like I'd pick the flavor of the week to focus on until I got bored and moved on to something else. All the while, I would share my feelings with others with my special blend of angst tinged with sarcasm.

This was my coping mechanism, though I will say that most people did not appreciate the artistry of it.

Love Revolution

At one point, I was so depressed I paid good money to go off to the desert in Arizona to beat pillows with a bat and recreate my birth. They say I was at the original event, but I'm not sure I did it justice. Suffice it to say, sitting in the arms of my replacement "parents" made me start to question many things in life.

It was at that retreat that I had a couple of "firsts." It was the first time someone told me that I didn't have to "do" anything to have value. This sounds absolutely crazy, but no one had ever said that to me before. You mean, I'm still worth something if I don't have the most important sounding job in D.C.? (Yes, I know how *that* sounds!)

The other "first" happened just from having a casual conversation with others at the retreat. I have no idea what I was even saying at the time, but I remember the reaction: "You should do stand-up!"

Whaaaaat? Uh yeah, ok, my persona is Depressed Person! Believe me, I am not trying to make you laugh, I am serious about feeling like shit! It was kind of my thing. Not to mention, I was kinda shy. I dislike the word shy, but that word was attached to me from birth.

OK, how shy were you? I was so shy as a child that I peed in my kindergarten chair. I was so shy, that my flute teacher from age eight told me that I did not speak for the first two months I took lessons from her! These were one-on-one lessons, so there was no one else in the room.

You get the picture. So, the idea that I would do stand-up comedy was ludicrous to me.

But the suggestion never completely went away. The frequency of people making the "stand-up" comment to me increased and I couldn't ignore it. I felt like I had something to say, and it had been pent up in me for decades.

I still couldn't see myself as "funny," though. So I took a "gateway drug" to stand-up - storytelling. I mean, who doesn't want to hear about my divorce? Anyone? No?

Yeah that's what I decided, too, as I took my first storytelling class. I heard about other people's kids, their traumatic diseases, their breakups, and I just didn't want to go there. Call it irony – I wanted people to listen to my sorrows, and then couldn't tell them.

So, I told a really dumb story about how I got pissed off about a commercial concerning frozen meat that I deemed misogynistic. Just go with me here.

The point is: people laughed. And not at me – at what I was saying.

Well maybe at me a bit. I have no idea.

But it felt like a coming-out of sorts. My friend told me that I'd found my calling. Well, what a relief because I'd been looking for that my entire life. The clouds parted.

OK, no they didn't. But I had to do stand-up after that taste of connecting with people, something I'd struggled with so much when I was younger. So of course, I took another class. There's a pattern here somewhere.

A class in stand-up – who knew there was such a thing? It must have been meant to be, if you believe in such things, because the class is so popular it sells out in minutes. But the minute I got the email, I signed up. I had committed to this, and there's nothing like putting money down to make you show up.

Every week the order we would perform in was chosen randomly. One week I got there right on the dot and was first up. There was zero time to think about it. This turned out to be a good thing – I torture myself with thinking, and worrying, and over-analyzing.

I'm usually super-sensitive to criticism. Yes, I know the point of a class is to learn, but don't tell me it feels good to be told you're not doing something right!

But I did OK. I didn't end up telling my life story onstage – I tried that later with mixed results.

I stuck to the ever-reliable subject of online dating for my stand-up, a synonym for emotional torture, so a good choice. When I would tell potential dates I did stand-up, they'd inevitably ask me, "Am I going to be in your act?" You wish, buddy, you wish.

The other students in the class ended up being very helpful. There's nothing like another set of eyes and ears to give you a completely different perspective on a punch line.

Then after about a month, it was show time! Granted it was all friends and family, but mostly other people's friends and family. I suppose this should have made it better. Not really.

The worst part, the absolute WORST part of stand up is waiting to go on. I was afraid I would forget everything. Don't ask me if anyone else was funny, because I couldn't tell you. I finally went backstage and it was time to go on. The wait was excruciating.

Finally, my name was called. It was all a bit unconscious after that. I'd rehearsed it so many times that I pretty much knew it. It's funny when you're so into a moment how it seems to go by so fast. But man, the laughs kept me going! After I was done, my brother and friend told me how great I was. I must say, I couldn't hear that enough.

Then the real test came – I was going to go out and really "do" stand up outside of the warm womb of my comedy class. It was a tough entry into the world.

I got my other brother and friends to come to some of my open mics, but how many times can you get people to do that? I'm an introvert. I have a limited friend list and some of these open mics told me to bring ten people? I don't have ten non-Facebook friends I could even ask.

I used the same material initially, but I started to get more personal with my depression. This got fewer laughs. I started to question it. The lowest point came on a Wednesday night in the basement of a very hot bar in D.C. I was sixteenth to go on. Yes, I said sixteenth. Oh, the glamorous world of stand-up open mics.

I guess you could call this my Dark Night of the Soul in stand-up comedy. My dad had passed away not two months before, so I hadn't been really feeling that funny. Yeah, I don't know why either.

But the family dynamics in my dad's passing just seemed like good material. So, there I am at 10 p.m. in that hot basement talking about being in the hospice with my sister. And no one laughs.

The hospice was just a setting, so it really wasn't about him dying. But when all I got was a weak chuckle, I couldn't get off that stage fast enough. I had to ask myself, why on earth am I torturing myself?

There was nothing fun about it, and everyone else was better than I was. And I clearly had no idea what millennials found funny. There is nothing millennial about me, except for the fact I feel like I've been alive for an entire one. I felt out of touch, old and beaten down. Not exactly the recipe for hilarity.

Everyone says you have to bomb when you do stand-up. But as in life, you have moments of, how much can I take? I know I did. I'm 40-something-or-other. What am I doing in a basement full of millennials?

My next thought was, "But am I really going to let a bunch of 20-somethings keep me down?" Perhaps the hospice story isn't the best material.

And anyway, my depression material did kind of get me a date. Another guy doing the show said that was his favorite part of what I did. Go figure. I'm never going to be everyone's cup of tea, this I know. But the ones who want my tea really have a taste for it!

The universe is funny. It kept giving me nudges to get back out there. I'd meet someone new, and they would say to me, "You should do stand-up." Honestly, I'm not even surprised anymore. But I had to be receptive to these messages to receive them.

So, if you're trying to figure out your path, take a bit of time for yourself at the beginning of each day. Close your eyes and just see what comes, but don't force it. You can call it meditation, or just tuning into yourself. You have access to your higher self, but you must quiet the mind to hear it.

And don't forget to write down what you learn! There's probably some great material in there for the greatest performance of all – your life.

Claire Geddes

Love At Work

"Power without love is reckless and abusive,
and love without power is sentimental and anemic.
Power at its best is love implementing the demands of justice,
and justice at its best is power correcting everything
that stands against love."
~Martin Luther King, Jr.

In some businesses these days, there is a revolution happening and it is fueled by love. It is creating work environments that are happier, healthier, profitable, and fun. Are you a part of this revolution?

Companies with happy employees outperform the competition by 20% and employees who are happy take ten times fewer sick days.[3] Happiness makes good business sense. The key is to allow yourself to be more in love, which is a doorway to happiness, meaningful work, innovation and so much more. Read on to discover the simple steps you can take today to join the uprising of Love At Work.

First, it is important to understand why love is important at work. A paradox exists in all work situations, whether you are self-employed or an employee of a multi-national corporation. The environment you work in defines the culture that shapes your mindset and behavior. At the same time, the people within your business create the culture and your ability to handle the challenges you face, whether internal or external. Is it individuals or systems that create happier work environments? It's *both* and it takes individuals grounded in love to develop healthy organizations that benefit *everyone* involved.

It is also important to see that happy and healthy work environments are possible. A recent Forbes article (2017) about Up&Up (a higher education marketing agency) is a great example. In the article Adam Landrum, the President & CEO said, "I used to think my employees' happiness was my number one priority. After a while of failing miserably, I learned I can't make them happy. Happiness is their responsibility." [4]

Adam needs to give himself credit for cultivating a culture of conscious and empowered leaders at his company as well as an "inspired workspace." Further, as CEO, he is setting the direction and intention to "harness team members' creative talent and help them create great work with one another."[4] It takes both empowered individuals and consistent leadership from the top to create healthy success like Up&Up is doing.

Let's take a closer look at what love has to do with happy work and why love is critical for both individuals and systems in creating healthy work environments.

Start by considering your current work situation. How do you feel about it? Are you willing to believe that it could be better that you can imagine? I invite you to open your mind as you read this article and tap into that place within you that knows. With love anything is possible. Stop this very moment, pause and without judgment, observe your breath.

Now take three deep and intentional breaths. Inhale love. Exhale peace. Three times, take a full deep breath and fully exhale. Let yourself relax, and simply be present and aware of your heart.

After creating space for presence within you, after feeling this new truth about what Love wants to bring you, think again about your work situation. How might it look different from a calmer outlook? Even a slight shift to a more centered and loving perspective opens doors of possibility.

> *"It is only with the heart that one can see rightly;*
> *what is essential is invisible to the eye."*
> *~ Antoine de Saint-Exupéry*

The root cause of *all* dysfunctional human interactions, in business and at home, is thinking based in fear and scarcity. This mindset creates an absence of trust and a fear of being vulnerable, which, according to speaker and author Patrick Lencioni, are the foundations of team dysfunction.

The good news is that there is a simple solution to this core issue and that is to shift into the calmer and more centered perspective of love. I know that this might still seem overly simplistic and maybe even impractical to you; if so, hang in there as we walk through some scenarios to see how this can work.

Most people struggle to maintain confidence about their value and worth, because we're human and because we live in an extremely complex and ever-changing world. As an individual, you must have an understanding of the value your work provides to make sure you're paid what you're worth. As a business, you must appreciate the value you bring to customers and what that's worth in the marketplace.

All people involved need to have a line of sight to the customer, so there is clarity about your value proposition: the unique benefits you provide a customer that solves a problem or improves a situation. How clear are you about the value you bring with your work? As things change, does that clarity sometimes get muddied?

Because of our capitalist society, we often confuse money and worth. Customary thinking has us believe that our value is determined by how much money we make. The problem with this tendency is that it relies on patterns of behavior that may or may not continue to be true: i.e., your worth in the past.

In addition, everyone has value, whether you're getting paid or not. To see beyond the limited perspective that money imposes, we must be able to individually see ourselves as gifted participants in creation. From the lens of fear and scarcity, we never do enough, have enough, or *are* enough. By contrast, from the lens of love and abundance, we are infinitely worthy, valuable, and creative. Love is the transformational energy that allows you to see your true importance, unrelated to money – "the place where your deep gladness and the world's deep hunger meet," as Frederick Beuchner said. Ironically, you will be free from money fears when you let Love show you your true worth.

A better determination of value than past earning history is your ability to love yourself and your gifts: who you are at your best and your ability to evolve and grow your awareness of these gifts. Yes, certain skills are more marketable than others. The bottom line is that self-love allows you to develop these skills upon a solid foundation of self-worth and connection to yourself and others.

> *"When our self-worth isn't on the line,*
> *we are far more willing to be courageous and*
> *risk sharing our raw talents and gifts."*
> *~ Brené Brown*

Love gives you the ability to objectively look at what I affectionately call drama: your doubts, fears, and weaknesses. Love allows you to see drama with compassion and vulnerability, as an aspect of your humanity, not as the definition of who you are, or of your value. From this perspective you can take 100% responsibility for your true gifts by sorting through the confusion and learning that drama provides. Love allows you to shift from a defensive posture to being open-minded and curious. To let go of the need to be right or please others, and to see the opportunities that are present in everyday life.

Love heals the root causes of dysfunction that lead to an absence of trust, in yourself and in others. Love leads to clarity about your true value and worth, and from these feelings, healthy and productive work environments can be built.

Another common workplace challenge is being overwhelmed. Demands to get more done in less time with fewer resources are omnipresent. The inclination to focus on results without considering relationships and process leads people to react without considering the priority of tasks, or whether they are actually the right person to get the work done. Working harder is valued over working smarter.

I recently had a client share frustration about how she and her colleagues were given awards for their heroic efforts to complete a construction project. But what she *really* wanted was a proactive and strategic effort to make the project run smoothly in the first place. When firefighting is what's validated, firefighting is what you'll get, and that shift to working smarter will never happen.

Once you start to become clear about your value, you can do something about being overwhelmed and operating with firefighting tendencies. Remember that, from the perspective of fear and scarcity, we never do enough, have enough, or *are* enough. From the perspective of love and abundance, we are infinitely worthy, valuable, and creative.

That means when you come from love, you're not wasting time and energy on drama. What becomes *more* important is staying true to yourself, your gifts, and what's right for *both* yourself and your organization. Otherwise you are not maximizing your value proposition. Love allows you to add working smarter to working hard, for yourself *and* for your customers, so the right work gets done by the right people; drama subsides and overwhelm ends.

> *"Energy, not time, is the fundamental currency*
> *of high performance."*
> *~ Jim Loehr*

How can you bring love to work and solve these challenges? The solution to these difficulties and so much more, is to pause, and observe your breath as I described above. This action causes a pattern interrupt in your fear-based biological reactions and allows time and space for your autonomic nervous system to calm down. You will tap into your gifts, the truth of your being, and the essence of life that is love. Sometimes this pause is very tricky; big feelings often lurk beneath your busy activities, feelings that you've been avoiding.

Love demands presence, both to your most precious talents and your deepest, darkest fears. The solution is not to deny your humanity; the solution is to bring love and compassion to your humanity and relentlessly take a stand for your gifts.

The proof of love at work is in the client stories we've collected over the years. We have many examples of people moving on to more lucrative work opportunities. One client in particular stands out: she doubled her salary in one job move. Yes, this person is an executive and was underpaid in her initial job. The fact is, she used the approach I've developed called the IAM Way. This method starts by anchoring into your best self. The executive was then able to know her true and unique value proposition and attract this profitable situation.

Many clients have also tamed the never-ending torment of being overwhelmed in its varied forms. Running short on time is often the biggest struggle people face. The IAM Way teaches people to take an abundance approach to time, and to focus more on managing their energy. Clients learn to pause, breathe, get more strategic, prioritize what's important, ask for help, and make progress on their most important work. As a result, project completion rates have soared.

Further, time is freed up to strategically create the culture, systems, and environments that lead to healthy success for all.

The first step to take is to be aware of whether your mindset is in fear or love, and then **choose love**. Use **the IAMx Map** as a guide, where True Self = love, and drama = fear:

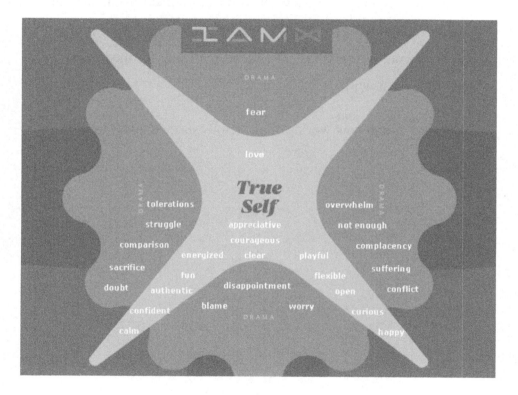

The IAM Way is a leadership approach that allows you to bring love to work. It creates the clarity, confidence and courage about your gifts to demonstrate that you need to be paid what you are worth. When you take a stand for these gifts, you'll experience more than enough time to get everything done and the end of overwhelm. The

Shangri La of work *is possible* in the present moment reality of love: happiness, meaningful work, creativity, and innovation. Even better, the IAM Way gives you a simple, repeatable, reliable, and effective process that is exactly the same for personal and business growth, so you can learn how to develop healthy cultures and systems. As a result, the love that emerges when you free yourself from fear can also be collectively aligned and leveraged to increase your profits and grow your business fast. We've been settling for mediocre performance at work.

With love, brand new worlds of audacious success await us!

Karen Tax

[3] Emil Shour, "11 Shocking Employee Happiness Statistics That Will Blow Your Mind," Snacknation, Oct, 23, 2015,
[4] Aileron, "Agree Or Disagree? Happiness Is Your Employees' Responsibility," Forbes, Nov 6, 2017.

Designing Your Dream Relationship: Compatibility Or Bust!

"Gauging up front how willing each of you are to bare your ass...
through sharing your dreams, your biggest desires
with both life and love, and – especially –
your biggest fears... and then doing just that,
is a crucial determinant of whether your relationship
will work out in the end."
~ Geoff Laughton

Who doesn't want more love? Anyone who says they don't is either lying or dysfunctionally protecting themselves. One of the ways we are able to practice getting and receiving love – as well as learning how you habitually keep love at a distance – is to get into a relationship. Yet, relationship is one of *the* most difficult things for a large majority of people to really figure out and get the hang of, which only makes sense when you consider how little, if any, training we get on how to do it well.

Through my own delightful and flawed marriage of 36 years, and from 21 years of working with couples as a Relationship Architect and coach, I've learned several all-too-common things that derail a relationship, but are preventable. I'm going to share variables that exponentially increase the odds that you can truly win at relationships. The first of these variables – by which you can predict whether a relationship is likely to go south or not – is all about how you get started.

Everyone gets into a relationship with the best of intentions and desires. When did you last get into a relationship thinking, "How awesome is it that I'm getting a chance to screw up yet another relationship and feel more miserable?" Yet, many people don't consider the importance of treating a relationship the same way you'd treat building a dream home, rather than flying by the seat of our pants. You would *never* build a dream house without a design, but people jump into relationships all the time with little to no design work done up front.

Consciously designing your relationship is an essential starting point for setting yourself up to co-create a *thriving* relationship, as opposed to the mediocre ones that far too many people settle for. Just as you want to make sure that your dream house is going to represent everything that's most precious to you in a home, you need to be sure that you're moving into a relationship that will bring you a lifetime (if it gets that far) of joy, challenge, growth, and – yes – mature love. The best design process to start with, that you really want to put the spotlight on first, is also one of the most overlooked and under-thought-of variables: assessing compatibility.

The traditional trajectory that I've seen in most relationships I've encountered – and it was certainly true with mine when we started – is that you meet somebody and there's an attraction, there's chemistry. Who doesn't love chemistry? The problem is that that chemistry is real and artificial at the same time. It *will* wear off, and you don't want to build a multi-year or lifetime relationship with somebody *just* on that. So, you need to explore and discover just how compatible you are or aren't!

While there are a *lot* of elements that go into compatibility, I'm focusing on three in particular here:

- Knowing what you want of, and from, a relationship.

- Knowing how you each relate to conflict.

- Knowing how compatible your core values are.

So, let's dive a little bit deeper into each of those.

When discussing what you want from a relationship, notice I didn't say, "What kind of partner do you want?" or "What do you want from a partner?" That all matters, absolutely, but unfortunately, if you start and stay *there*, no matter how often you meet somebody who looks like they're filling that bill, you still have a high chance of having a lot of unpleasant and destructive surprises that unfold along the way.

You must be very clear about what you want *from* a relationship from the start. Another way of saying this is, "*Why* do you want a relationship?"

A lot of people will answer that question with something along the lines of, "Well, I want a companion," or "I want an in-house cheering section that'll always be in my camp and will be there for me unconditionally," etc. That's all fine and good, but it isn't enough. This is looking to the outside to fill a need that can only be met internally. So, if that's the main criterion, you're setting yourself up for an unhealthily co-dependent, rather than inter-dependent, relationship.

It's crucial to know why you want a relationship, what you want from it, and what you want the relationship to serve, besides your own heart, needs, wants, and desires. You want to really learn as much as possible about that for yourself and the other person *early on*. Keep in mind, too, that where you start won't be where you end up, because a great relationship will always be oriented to life-long growth. Even the *purpose* of relationship evolves. What I saw as the purpose of my marriage is very different now, at 60, than it was when I was 24. You've got to design your foundation from what you both require, because if you want fundamentally different things, that may not necessarily be a complete deal-breaker, but it's damn close to one.

Let's shift now to the next compatibility variable to assess: relationship to conflict. Conflict is a *really* hot issue and mission-critical for *any* relationship, not just romantic ones. It's such a key component of any thriving relationship. In my last book, *How to Build a Conflict-Proof Relationship,* a central premise is that the point is *not* to avoid or prevent conflict. That's a death sentence for a relationship. If you and the other person are both committed to that, you would be compatible in a dysfunctional way. Rather than avoiding conflict, you both have got to learn how to get really great at it. And to do so *consciously.*

Conflict is *essential* – let me repeat: essential – to any healthy relationship. The problem is most of us just don't know how to do it very well, and most of us didn't have good models to teach us as we were growing up. All our initial modeling and "training" came from our families during childhood. Oh boy!

When you want to make that leap from casual dating to really designing a committed relationship with each other, you need to ask each other a few key questions. The first is, "How do you feel and think about conflict?" As you ask that, you want to watch each other's body language, facial expressions, and the ease (or lack thereof) that they (and you) have answering the question. For example, the other person might say, "Conflict? Yeah...I guess conflict's okay." Or, "I *love* conflict! I eat it for lunch. How about you?!"

Depending on who you are, either of those answers could be problematic, but you've each *got* to know your visceral stand on the issue. If you don't know whether you have fundamentally opposing beliefs and perspectives, that gets to be very tough to overcome. Not completely impossible, but as close to impossible as I know. You want to notice how present each of you can be with the questions and answers. When you talk about it, you'll also get a fairly quick read about how willing you are to be vulnerable, transparent, and present. Those each matter, because you need all three to be a conflict – and conflict resolution – ninja!

Share how your parents handled conflict when you were growing up (or not). Did they hide (or at least try to) their conflicts and never, ever fight in front of you? Or, did they let their conflicts run roughshod over the whole family, leaving everyone shell-shocked? Either approach will create huge challenges in how you're going to relate to conflict, and you each want to know that up front early on. It's important to really gauge history and its impact on your current attitudes and practices around conflict.

Lastly, you really need to boldly share your own relationship histories. What I knew about conflict when I was in my teens and

20s was generally to stay the hell away from it at any cost. In my family, conflict was frequent, nasty, and, if anything, set a model for why one *wouldn't* want to be in a relationship.

So, a quick story here to illustrate the value of this. On my first date with Sarah, I wanted to make an amazingly great impression on her, spurred by her being older than me. The pressure was on me not to seem immature to her. Within the first half hour of our date, some of the hot chocolate I was drinking went down the wrong pipe, and I ended up coughing up hot chocolate…all over her brand-new suit and white blouse!

"Oh shit!" I thought.

For me, I'd sunk the ship before it ever left port. If I'd done that at the dinner table at home, I would've been yelled at, shamed, and made to feel like an idiot. When Sarah responded with a laugh, and even went out of her way to try to make me feel better about it, I learned then and there that whenever the going got rough, I'd be met with enormous compassion…a hypothesis that has proven to be true the majority of times over the years. That actually broke the ice, and we both shared an enormous amount about our past relationships (in her case, a past marriage), and all that we saw we'd contributed to their failures.

When things come up that scare you (about you or them), *share* that! If you see red flags, either in your attitudes or theirs, you must talk about those. See if you can find some common ground on believing truly and sincerely, as I do, that conflict is a growth path, not a problem.

This will provide each of you, and your relationship, with healing and growth opportunities. If your prospective partner doesn't want any of that, then you'll know up front that you're likely incompatible. ***If you're not compatible, you can't force or manufacture it.*** *That* is essential to remember. Ignore it at your own peril.

Let's finish by looking at values. Having compatible values is *just* as important. Why? Because values really are fundamental – they're like our operating system. You can be compatible with someone who has *some* variations that complement yours. But, it's pretty hard to have Mac and Windows be truly compatible. You need to deeply explore all this with each other.

For example, if you must live in a rural area and they – even with so much juicy sex and *seeming* compatibility – really must live in a city, you're going to have a fundamental values conflict. Value priorities on money, religion/spirituality, politics, etc. are critical to discover, along with the shockingly under-discussed topic of what your values are regarding children (having them or not) and parenting. I've seen relationships destroyed, years after the fact, because of extreme values conflicts in this area.

You should know, *before* committing to a relationship, what your key relationship *and* life values are, and where there are conflicts. You need to see if these can be resolved and/or bridged, early on… *if* you want to set your relationship up to win.

While this is far from an exhaustive list of do's and don'ts, this gives you basic steps for how to successfully evaluate compatibility during the design stage of things. If you share early on – *and throughout your relationship* – you can both keep from staying tightly wedded to a rigid and/or delusional picture of who you each are, and what your relationship can be. This can prevent stagnation and staleness that will suffocate your relationship from within.

Geoff Laughton

The Art Of Attraction Alchemy

"Vulnerability sounds like truth and feels like courage.
Truth and courage aren't always comfortable,
but they're never weakness."
~ Brené Brown

Imagine waking up in the morning, and the first thing that you hear from your husband next to you are the words, "I love you." He then snuggles up even closer to you. After that, you meditate together in bed before you do your individual affirmations. This describes my morning every day.

Now imagine, it's the middle of the day, and you are working, and something is triggering you. Instead of reacting, your partner lovingly asks you what's coming up for you and helps you to process your emotions.

But not only that, he then asks you if there is more that wants to come out or be expressed. He fully sees you, hears you and feels you. You feel so safe with him, and this allows you to see past your projections and walls and see your fears transformed.

Imagine that every part of you truly feels safe, loved and welcomed. Imagine that you can skip, be silly, be loud, sing, dance all you want, and your partner absolutely loves it.

However, it wasn't always like this for me. Freedom and safety were not ways I would describe my early life.

I grew up in a German household with an emotionally unavailable mother, and an emotionally abusive father. And in this household those same words, "I love you," or hugs, were as common as Christmas and Thanksgiving happening on the same day.

Fast forward many years later, and as I became an adult and began dating, what do you think I began to attract? That's right – "Emotionally Unavailable Men!" I soon began to feel the pangs of loneliness, frustration, sadness and isolation caused by this, and very soon I had had enough.

I decided to pack up my bags and to take the biggest risk of all. To leave Germany and move to the United States to study Personality Psychology at U.C. Berkeley. I wanted to finally uncover why the type of relationship that I had with my parents growing up was directly correlated with my life-long dating & relationship struggles with men.

While I did this, I also began studying everything that I could get my hands on in the areas of men, dating, personality styles and interpersonal communication and relationships. I went to dozens and dozens of workshops and training programs on these subjects, read hundreds of books, and spent over ten thousand dollars on this to create my new dream life and dream love into a reality. I even began leading "Soulmate Support Groups" to help other women start finding success in their love lives. And guess what? It was working for them!

Although I had started to help dozens of other single women attract the boyfriends, fiancées & husbands of their dreams with the wisdom, strategies and systems that I had learned, it still wasn't happening for me. Finally, I came to the realization that it wasn't working for me because I was so "stuck in my own patterns" that I couldn't see the forest for the trees... And that's when I finally decided to hire a professional dating coach and relationships mentor for myself.

This coach was quite an investment financially, and I was scared about it at first, but I knew that this is what I had to do if I ever wanted anything to change with my own dating and romantic life. And after working with my dating coach and mentor for just a few months, I finally broke through. I finally learned how to trust myself and my own heart in my decision making, how to believe in myself. I found that this was all possible for me and that I deserved to have what I wanted.

I learned how to step out of my comfort zone and to take massive new risks in my life without fear. I learned how to say "Yes" to letting the new love and support finally flow to me and not push it away subconsciously with the old fear and safety patterns that were keeping me stuck and alone.

Shortly after that breakthrough happened, I finally was able to attract my amazing, loving and supportive husband into my life. We have now been married for $3^1/_2$ years, and couldn't be happier, traveling, growing, loving and helping to create a better and more loving world to live in for generations to come.

Through this entire journey which led to attracting true love into my life where previously there was only struggle and heartbreak, I became so passionate about helping other successful women to magnetize the man to share their life with. To be happier without loneliness, frustration, sadness or wasting any more life, time and energy!

Having said that, allow me now to share with you three of my best secrets (with the help of my amazing husband Brody) to start magnetizing the man to share your life with and be happier quickly!

Let's begin with powerful secret #1!

SECRET #1 – BE VULNERABLE WITHOUT FEELING WEAK

Sounds simple, doesn't it?

What we mean here is that you should start cultivating the courage within yourself to lean in and be vulnerable. Open yourself up and share your deepest and darkest thoughts and fears with the men that you want to develop a strong relationship with.

Brody and I did a shadow ceremony the night before our wedding where we shared the most insecure feelings and fears we had toward each other and toward the idea of marriage and a long-term relationship. In that night, I found out that Brody, as a recovered "emotionally unavailable man," was afraid to be trapped. I was afraid that I wasn't good enough for him since in my opinion he has it all and was the perfect man. He has the looks, the talent and is an incredible lover as well.

You see, we make up all those stories in our heads about why we don't deserve a partner or why we are not worthy of being treated lovingly and cherished.

Of course, the part of us who fears these things is a very young part of us and is afraid to feel inadequate. So instead of feeling shame around that, I exposed that deepest fear that I had to my husband and he did the same for me. From this point on we could actually communicate to each other's value system, meaning that we could create a marriage in which each and every one of our different "parts" inside had a voice and was listened to.

On the day of our wedding, we then also told each other "With this ring I set you free," which made the part of my husband that was afraid of being controlled able to feel safer going into our marriage. Now what did we mean by that statement? How can you be "free" within a life-long commitment, you might ask?

Simple. It's called "healthy inter-dependence." I am an absolute advocate for my husband taking time by himself. This could be going on a walk by himself or taking a day to be by himself. For example, Brody loves to go to the zoo and I don't. I maintain a fierce stand for the part inside of him that can only be fed in solitude.

Brody is freer in our marriage than he was on his own because that independent part has another cheerleader on his team. Me!

Brody then allows the part inside of me that is afraid of not being good enough to feel safe by regularly showing me how much he loves me and cares about me and that he will never "leave" no matter how intense things might get.

SECRET #2 - INCREASE YOUR CAPACITY TO ALLOW A MAN TO SUPPORT YOU

So many ladies come to me and tell me they want to be more supported by their chosen man. But do they really? Being supported means letting go of control. And how well has that been going for you?

In my Discovery Sessions with the hundreds of women who've come to me, we usually discover that they have a very hard time allowing a man to take control and to be the "masculine leader" in the relationship. In other words, allowing him to be their "hero."

How long does it take until you take the wheel of control from your man? I know you are a successful woman, accomplished in your own right and the last thing you need is a man telling you what to do, right?

However, in order for a man to truly be able to emotionally, mentally, physically and spiritually support you, you must allow him to take that lead. A more masculine man who wants to be your protector, provider, lover and hero will only be drawn and attracted to you when you can make him feel needed and allow him to step into that role fully.

This method does not necessarily have to be financial. It is usually emotional. I invite you to lean into the un-comfort to feel vulnerable and to open up your heart to receive this love, attention and support from the amazing men out there who want to give it to you, if only you would be open enough to truly see it and receive it long-term.

SECRET #3 - TAKE OWNERSHIP AND RESPONSIBILITY TO INCREASE YOUR CONFIDENCE AND CONNECTION

The secret to confidence lies in your ability to trust in your capacity to take responsibility and ownership for your life. When we blame and shame ourselves, trust goes downhill, and with that goes our self-confidence.

When you blame your partner or men in general, then there is nothing that you can do about it.

It's outside of your realm of influence, and with that your ability to create your reality. Besides, everything you project, you perceive. Meaning, the more you blame others, the more you will find reasons to blame others. It becomes a vicious cycle that keeps you and your partner disconnected and inauthentic.

Even worse, this pattern of self-protection and giving your power away leads to resentment and trading for love versus generously sharing it. Every time our responsibility decreases, so does our confidence. Confidence in and of itself describes the capacity to deal with any challenge that comes your way, meaning you have all the resources inside of yourself and that you are an infinitely resourceful being.

Picture this: You are in a relationship and you feel the passion is missing. Now, you could blame your partner for the passion not being there, or you could ask yourself, "How can I bring even more passion into the relationship?" Or you could ask "How can I create even more space for passion to happen in our relationship"?

Which approach do you feel is more likely to lead towards creating the life and relationship that you desire? As you sow, so shall you reap.

Once you take full responsibility for all the results in your romantic life, once you give up the right to blame the world, men or your chosen man, and take new action and new risks, you can start creating the lasting, loving relationship of your dreams. Only then does a whole new world of possibility in love open up to you for you to claim.

Those are our 3 secrets to help you start magnetizing the man to share your life with. They will help you to be happier ASAP without loneliness, frustration or wasting any more time!

Remember, dreams can come true!

Antia and Broderick Boyd

Love Revolution

Learning To Love
In The 21st Century

"Love is always open arms. If you close your arms about love you will find that you are left holding only yourself."
~ Leo Buscaglia

Women today want to find love but a seismic shift in society has changed the relational landscape.

Although change is good, it also brings about uncertainty and lack of clarity in how to approach the new normal. What I often end up seeing in my practice are angry women and resentful men and nobody knows exactly why they feel that way.

Why has something so primal and essential become so confusing and messy?

Political correctness makes talking about male/female relationships feel like walking on a tightrope.

However, the flow of conversation changes if we pivot to yin and yang energy instead.

LOVE TIP #1: KNOW HOW YOU FEEL LOVED

How you feel loved is based on your individual Yin-Yang Energetic Template.

Every single one of us, man and woman alike, is a psychological hybrid of yin (feminine) and yang (masculine) energy.

However, our sex does not necessarily determine our Energetic Template. A man may be predominantly yin energy, a woman predominantly yang energy. And each of us is a mix of both energies, some more fluid than others.

Yin energy is feeling-oriented, emotional, vulnerable, mercurial, correlating with the hormone estrogen. Also associated with yin energy are being passive, patient, receptive, available, open, and respectful of those who provide pleasure and who take care of our feelings.

If you are predominantly yin energy, having your feelings cherished is how you feel respected.

Complementary to yin is yang.

Yang energy is action-oriented, competitive, conquering, controlling, and correlates with the hormone testosterone. Also associated with yang energy are logic, analysis, giving, protecting, and cherishing those who respect one's judgment.

If you are predominantly yang energy, you feel loved by being respected.

Yin respects yang. Yang feels loved.

Yang cherishes yin. Yin feels respected.

This cycle allows you both to get cherished and respected, which is important for your relationship's peace and ultimate success.

Before learning this information, I struggled. Often feeling unheard, I kept trying to "explain" my feelings. In doing so, I ended up in logical battles with men about my feelings. Ultimately, my attempts at understanding ended up in battles for control.

In my view, I wanted to be understood. In his eyes, I wanted him to agree.

Rather than continue to be logical about my feelings, I needed to say what I was feeling. And stop.

Feelings aren't debatable.

Being accepted while feeling my feelings was what I really needed.

But, I didn't learn that until my 40's.

A HUGE shift materialized in my relationships when I internalized these changes into my life.

After waiting many years for the right man and for me to be the right woman, I'm now married to a loving, generous man who hears what I'm feeling and holds space for me at the same time.

CONSCIOUSLY ENTERING INTO A RELATIONSHIP

When you enter into a relationship, it's critical to make a conscious decision about which party wants to be primarily the yin and who wants to be primarily the yang energy in the relationship.

Yes – you can be fluid and go back and forth, but this will make your communication more challenging.

What happens when you don't decide in advance?

Well, if you're like my client Caroline, who wants both to be respected and cherished, you'll end up competing all the time and then wonder why your feelings aren't being taken care of.

When Caroline first came to me she'd been active on dating apps, going out at least once a week and sometimes up to three times a week. Intermittently, she was excited by a prospect, then exhausted and ready to give up.

After some work, Caroline realized that at the end of the day, when coming home to her partner, she'd rather be hugged if she was feeling bad, helped to feel better if she didn't feel good or celebrated if things were going well.

Having her feelings taken care of, she discovered, was more important to her than having her thoughts respected. She would rather the man made plans for the evening, made any decisions or suggestions, and he could ask her how she felt about it. That felt good to her.

Making the decision to change, and actually changing, however, are two different things.

We worked together on enhancing her communication skills, debriefing after her dates, and were often in contact during texting conversations.

She mastered how not to squabble over little things that didn't matter, like whether something actually happened last Tuesday or "no, it was Wednesday." She learned how not to give directions while he was driving, unless he asked for her help.

These slight changes and more made huge differences in how the men she dated perceived her and how she felt on dates. Now she was sitting back, more confident and yet more relaxed. She was allowing men to entertain her rather than sitting on the edge of her seat feeling like she had to make sure everything was running smoothly.

On a night Caroline was out shopping with a girlfriend, Joshua saw her and felt compelled to walk over and talk to her. He told her that she was radiant that day (and really every day since) and he couldn't let the moment go by.

Together now for three years, married for over a year, they are happy, in love, and can't believe they found each other.

And they're both in the energetic role they want to be in.

LOVE TIP #2: IT'S OK TO WANT TO BE IN A RELATIONSHIP

I can't count the number of clients who've said to me something along the lines of *"I don't have to be in a relationship. I'm fine without one. But I guess it would be nice to have one…someone to do something with on weekends, to come home to at night, to lie in bed next to."*

The follow up statement is some philosophical rant about how "you're born alone, you die alone," an abstract reason for steering clear of relationships for now.

The thing is…this philosophy isn't true.

You are not born alone.

We are born into relationship.

There is no mother without child; no child without mother.

Doctors now accept what villagers instinctively knew before Western medicine got in the way.

Newborn babies are now often placed on the mother's chest to promote immediate bonding, skin to skin, face to face, smell to smell, eye to eye, and voice to voice.

Similarly, from the moment we start to seek a romantic relationship, we look for the same bonded feeling. We search for the look in someone's eye that says *"I will be here for you always, no matter what. You are the most important person in the world to me."*

How we relate to that person has so much to do with how we related to our opposite-gendered parent.

For instance, Sheryl had a father who provided for her physical needs but did not provide for her emotional needs. When Sheryl was born, her father had wanted a boy, so he had taught her what he wanted her to know:

- Think logically, not with emotions.

- Don't let people see you're weak or vulnerable; don't cry.

- Know how to act in the business world; shake a man's hand firmly and look him in the eye.

So, when Sheryl started dating she didn't realize that a man taking care of her feelings or protecting her was something a man could, should or would provide.

Instead, Sheryl took care of everything. She often approached the man, starting the conversation. If he didn't ask, she'd suggest, "Let's exchange phone numbers." If she didn't hear from him by the next day, she'd call him that night.

When she went out on a date, she had no problem picking up the check and proposing they get together again. She would often send a text after the date saying she had a good time.

If, for the second date, the guy suggested "Why don't you come by my house?" he literally just had to open his door. That was it. Nothing. He had to do nothing at all.

Sheryl was not happy. She didn't want to be in these non-relationships anymore, but she didn't know how to change what was happening.

She created this persona of being "OK" with being single but she *so* wasn't OK.

She questioned everything. "Will I ever find the right guy? Is there someone out there for me? How come it's happened for my friends and not for me?"

She admitted that she even looked at people on the streets who she didn't know, wondering how they got together. Secretly, feeling "better than" on the one hand, and "less than" on the other, she felt horribly judgmental and insecure all at the same time.

Getting Sheryl comfortable admitting to herself that she wanted an interdependent, secure relationship, which is a healthy, normal human experience, was the first layer of peeling off her mask.

Having her admit it to others was the next layer.

But disclosing this to the men she dated meant she had to get truly intimate.

LOVE TIP #3: THE TRUTH ABOUT INTIMACY
Intimacy is the ability to say what you are thinking and feeling in the moment you are thinking and feeling it in a way that the other person can hear it.

Imagine not having to run every thought and feeling through some filtering mechanism in your brain, wondering how the other person will receive it.

That thought is either liberating or frightening.

Once you are able to get there and actually do it, what a feeling of freedom and connection!

Now, mash-up freedom and connection and what do you have? Total acceptance.

This sense of total acceptance and connection is the basis of how you'll be secure enough as a couple to be independent in the world, yet completely interdependent in your relationship.

Losing that connection feels like a baby feels losing connection with its mother. Fear, panic, confusion, pain…

In an intimate, stable, healthy relationship, we make sure the other person feels our love, acceptance, presence, and support.

When we first started working together, Sheryl was anxious about admitting that she didn't want to stay single any longer. Fortuitously, we'd worked out some of those butterflies before she met Loren.

Sheryl was prepared when Loren asked why she was "still single." She divulged that she was looking for her life-long companion.

Loren surprised Sheryl when he said he was too.

As they continued to date, Sheryl challenged herself to remain open and to voice her feelings in the moment, rather than censor herself as she'd done in the past.

Loren told Sheryl he was looking for a woman who'd have his back; he'd have hers, and who would be in this for the long run.

Ultimately, Loren and Sheryl have gotten married and are blissfully happy.

LOVE REVOLUTION

We want to start a love revolution. NOW IS THE TIME.

When we balance our masculine and feminine energy in a relationship, it's like dancing the Texas Two-Step. And, having lived in Texas, I've seen two people who've just met dance it exquisitely, where it looks like they've choreographed the dance in advance.

But perhaps even MORE awe-inspiring is to imagine panning out from a crowded dance floor filled with competent dance partners. The couples dance and twirl without hitting or bumping into each other.

If everyone has healthy, balanced masculine and feminine energies flowing effortlessly between them, and the world's energy would flow. Balance and harmony in any relationship can exist: lovers, spouses, families, friends, co-workers.

The confusion and messiness would be gone.

All our relationships have the possibility of feeling good, right, and balanced.

And, nonetheless, it starts with one.

Most importantly still is finding that person who fills that need to be our one and only; the one person who will look into our eyes and say, "You are the most important person in the world to me."

Dr. Sharon Cohen

Stop Looking Outside Yourself For Love

"Loving ourselves works miracles in our lives."
~ Louise L. Hay

After spending 15 years with "Mr. Wrong," at age 36, I finally found "Mr. Right." His name was Dann (yes, with two "n's.") It was love at first sight – we liked the same activities, the same foods, we had similar backgrounds, and the same wacky sense of humor.

We'd go running together, shared a love of all things chocolate, dark beer, and we talked non-stop. He was my knight in shining armor and he treated me like I was his princess. He fixed things around my house without being asked, he'd buy me cute little presents, and he was always a gentleman.

He had a couple of skeletons in his closet, but who doesn't? I decided it didn't matter. He also had a history of depression and I "knew" if I loved him enough, he wouldn't need to go down that dark road again. Everything was wonderful. Several of my girlfriends were envious that their partners didn't treat them as well as Dann treated me.

After we had been together for just over a year, Dann suffered a workplace injury. He was descending a ladder on a very windy day, and was grasping the ladder when the wind caught it. He held tightly onto the ladder to stop it hitting overhead hydro wires. In the process, he herniated two discs in his back.

After this incident Dann was off work for a long time. He attempted many different forms of treatment, both traditional and holistic. We were already engaged to be married and went ahead with our wedding three months after Dann's accident. He was still very loving, and we were so happy together.

Over the course of the next couple of years, after dealing with the bureaucracy of The Workplace Safety & Insurance Board, Dann's herniated discs were not healing. He was denied as a candidate for back surgery. After this, Dann's demeanor, and indeed his personality, changed. He was seeing pain specialists without much relief and he saw a family doctor who did psychological counseling.

He was using pain medication, psychiatric drugs and alcohol to numb both his physical and emotional pain. He slowly stopped seeing all his holistic practitioners, concluding that they weren't helping (despite improvements in his physical condition) and that they cost too much money given that he wasn't able to work.

After the orthopedic surgeon told him that he was not a candidate for back surgery (something that Dann had decided would be his "saving grace"), he went into a fast and deep downward emotional spiral. He was angry a lot of the time. He withdrew from friends and family and he started communicating with me less and less.

One Sunday evening after cleaning up the dinner dishes, I noticed Dann walking back up our driveway from the road. He had moved my car onto the road and was heading towards his car. I knew he shouldn't be driving as he'd been "self-medicating" with a fair amount of beer that day. I ran out to the driveway and asked him what he was doing. He said that he was going for a drive to crash his car and kill himself. He'd had enough of living with chronic pain.

I pulled his car keys out of his hand and told him that he wasn't killing himself "on my watch." I also said that chances were if he was in his car, he'd hurt or kill someone else too. To say that he was angry is an understatement. He walked down the street with me in tow. I was so afraid he was going to throw himself into traffic or find "another way."

He realized I wasn't relenting so he eventually turned around and walked back home. As we walked up the front steps to enter the front door, Dann turned and looked at me with such an anguished combination of despair and hatred that it caught me by surprise.

He spat out the words, "F*&k you" and entered the house to spend the rest of the evening sitting in the living room with me and talking very little. In hindsight I maybe should have called the police to take him to the hospital for suicide watch. I really don't know. I know I was in shock and in denial. A part of me thought he didn't really mean it, that he was just crying for help.

He actually got up for work the next morning almost as if the previous evening hadn't happened. He had acquired a job as a manager of a self-storage facility fairly recently and he didn't want to mess that up, given that I had foiled his evening's plans. He promised not to attempt to take his life again.

After that, he continued to grow more sullen and withdrawn. His amazing sense of humor was gone. He told me on several occasions that I deserved better than him and that he really thought he should move out. He was worried that, with his anger level, he might physically hurt me someday. I never really thought he would.

About a month later he told me he'd found a one-bedroom apartment and that he was moving out in two weeks. Two weeks! I was dumbfounded. I didn't think he'd actually leave. I thought it was just talk. The "old" Dann was going to come back to the way he used to be – I was sure of it. He just needed more time to heal and to return to his old self again.

Dann did move out and he didn't return to his old self. We stayed in almost daily email or phone communication for a while. I went to his apartment at least weekly for dinner and he would come to the house occasionally as well. After about six months, I realized that he couldn't handle the "stress" of living with me, or anyone else for that matter. He wasn't coming back. I felt like I had failed him and our marriage. I hadn't been able to heal him or help him cope with his depression or his physical pain.

Over time our communication decreased to about once a week and then to about once a month. About two years after he left, Dann was at my house for dinner and he said that his back pain was worse than ever. He told me he had slipped a few months prior on a patch of ice outside his apartment building. A few months prior to that, he'd been let go from his job – his anger had come out a few too many times at work. His family doctor advised him to apply for a disability pension as she didn't think he'd be able to work again. This destroyed his sense of self-worth.

Two weeks after this visit I received an email from Dann that was sent to numerous friends. It read, "So long and thanks for all the fish." This is a line from "Hitchhiker's Guide to the Galaxy." It's a "departing" remark. By the time I saw the email, several hours had passed since Dann had sent it. The e-mail had an ominous tone and I called his cell phone right away. His voicemail picked up. I then called his new girlfriend's cell phone and left her a message.

Yes, he actually had a girlfriend despite all his "issues"– a woman he'd been seeing for about six months. I thought perhaps the two of them had an argument or maybe even broke up, given his worsened state. I hoped she could shed some light on the situation. I kept calling both of them the next day with no response.

On the second day I called his apartment superintendent and asked if they could go into his apartment to check on him. Of course, they couldn't do that legally. I told them I was calling the police. I did call the police and, at first, they didn't want to do anything. After all, I was "the ex-wife."

They also didn't understand the strange email and how that could be indicative of someone possibly harming themselves. I convinced them to inspect his apartment. When they reached his building, the police officer called me again. Was I sure there was the possibility that Dann could have harmed himself? Dammit, yes, could they please go in and check on him?!! They said that they would and that they'd call me back.

They didn't call me back. Two hours later, two uniformed police officers, a male and female, came to my office. I met with them in a boardroom where they informed me that Dann was indeed in his apartment and he was no longer living. Part of me already knew he was gone and part of me was in a state of disbelief.

I had to give a statement to the officers. They were very kind to me during the whole process.

I was numb for days following. I was also really angry at Dann. Not only for killing himself, but for giving up. I realize now that was a huge judgment on my part. I had no idea, really, what he was going through, either physically or emotionally, and it was not my place to judge him or his actions.

The passage of time has allowed me to see that Dann chose the only option that he saw was available to him at that time to release both his physical and emotional pain.

I can also see that it wasn't my job to "fix" him. I always felt like I had failed him somehow by not finding a way to alleviate his pain. I introduced him to different holistic modalities and after trying them and even though he had experienced some great results, he rejected them.

I used to think...if only I had loved him more, I could have saved him.

Now I see that I did love him enough. That love had changed after he left, over time, to the love that one has for a dear friend. I also see now that he loved me and wanted to spare me from being with the person he had become. He had loved me, but he hadn't loved himself.

We must allow love to change and evolve when it's required.

I can now be grateful for the person Dann was, even when he "changed." I can also be in allowance of his choice. Without that allowance, I could not heal.

I also learned to be grateful for me and not to make myself wrong for "choosing" him. That is truly a precious gift – to never feel we are wrong for the choices we make. I invite you to look at all the places and events in your life where you have made yourself wrong and turn the "wrongness" into gratitude. Yes, even the things that you think are horrible.

Gratitude is one of the biggest healers and creators of love that there is. Be grateful for the things that are good and be grateful for the things that are "bad" because even in the "bad" there is something to be learned or it can be a catalyst for something greater in your life.

You cannot live your life for or through someone else. Not your parents, your partner, your kids, your friends. We can't look to someone else to complete us or to make us feel whole or happy. That's something we must do for ourselves.

You must live your life for you. If you don't, you'll never be happy. If you live for someone else, you will end up being resentful. Only when your cup is full of love for yourself can it overflow with love for others.

Love Revolution

Another important lesson I learned is to never wait to go after your dreams. Go after them NOW. You never know if there is going to be a tomorrow.

Love yourself like there is no tomorrow.

Kim Louise Morrison

The Beat

"When life shows itself to be tumultuous,
it's because you are being prepared for something greater."
~ Usher

Return to Love after Loss...

The future stands open-armed in an invitation,
Each step a lifetime's journey
In and out, into myself.
Who I am and who I might become.

Courage doesn't mean anything without purpose and direction.
My life extends far beyond the limitations of me but,
If I were to remain invisible My truth would stay hidden!
Love endures eternity and repeats itself endlessly thru eons of
lessons.
Will they ever believe one can make a difference -
That a single drop in a sea of unconsciousness will awaken them
all?

I was walking down a wide hallway lined with books when out of the corner of my eye, I caught a movement on one of the top shelves. Turning to look, I was shocked to see myself sitting up there, knees crossed, with the top leg bouncing in that anxious way I sometimes caught myself sitting. Looking closer, I watched "me" give me a quizzical look as if to say, "What the hell am I doing up here again?" Then I really heard, "Get off this damned shelf!"

A lot of us find ourselves at a crossroads in our lives when we just aren't sure what we want to do or which way to turn. We just know that as happy as our lives appear from the outside looking in, they may not be. At least from our insides looking out, it doesn't feel that way.

When you reach that point of no more indecision and begin your search for something different, where do you start? How do you go on? How do you step back into life consciously? How do you say yes to living your life, intentionally?

The year 1999 was one of my light bulb years. I turned fifty and was gifted the book Medicine Woman by a friend. I loved it and began to read all of Lynn Andrews' books as the great stories they were. I had no clue the teachings these stories held and how they would change, even save, my life in the years to come.

I struggled to find a purpose for my life and a way to reconnect with my marriage. It all seemed so far away. I was stuck. In reality, I was on a treadmill running with the proverbial hamsters in a constant state of movement. I had never designed my life for living. It was designed for doing. I was living a full-blown reactive life, not a purpose-filled one.

Peeling back the layers of what was then, I began to look at what I wanted life to be moving forward. I was in desperate need of a purpose, a way to live more fully as me, not just as a mom, wife, daughter, sister, Realtor, advocate or friend.

I needed to learn how to truly live with me, to live intentionally each day, even in each moment, with each decision I made. I wanted to live and move through life gracefully. I read about this thing called the Law of Deliberate Creation. It is the purposeful focusing of thought with the intention of feeling alignment with one's own desire. I took this idea to heart and slowly began to intentionally create the life I wanted to live.

I became aware of my own deepest desires, searched out my own dreams and sense of worth and value. I began to see each day as an opportunity to choose who and how I wanted to be in the world, to take responsibility for my own dreams and to walk truthfully with all those that shared my life.

I found teachers, classes, events, and schools to attend. Boy, I got busy (something I was really good at doing). I read and wrote and circled myself in a way I never knew existed. I made a commitment to try to live each day intentionally, to mindfully choose where I would exert time and energy, and what thoughts would fill my mind. I picked up the reins of my own life. I moved into the driver's seat, knowing that I held the key to getting off the shelf and back into a life of living consciously!

I began to dream big. I was designing my own destiny, welcoming resistance as an opportunity. I heard that often still voice once again as it pulled on my heart. "There's more you know," I heard it whisper. "Get off the shelf!"

It takes courage to make changes. I love what Mary Ann Radmacher says, "Courage doesn't always roar. Sometimes courage is the quiet voice at the end of the day saying, 'I will try again tomorrow.'"

When 2005 came, I was well into my spiritual journey. My husband and I were dating and making time for each other. We were out of debt, both kids were out of college and married, life was good, and I loved it again.

I was driving home from Colorado with my daughter when the call came. A voice on the other end of the line cried out, "Ryan's ... there's been..." a mumbled voice tried to tell me something... "What's happened?" I cried. And the voice on the phone flatly said, "He's dead!"

I slammed into a place of survival mode with the loss of our son in a freak accident. Ryan and I had been chatting not more than twenty or thirty minutes earlier, and his last words to me on the phone before it happened were, "I've gotta go, Mom!" Then he hung up.

I woke up the morning Ryan was to be cremated with an intense need to hold him again. I called the mortuary and made an appointment for one last visit. As I hugged his cold, still-hearted body for the last time, my hand began to tap a drumbeat that resonated through his hollow chest. He had called me to him for a final gift. Ryan gave me a song and a drum beat to use on those nights when I couldn't sleep. I would tap the mattress with my fingertips and as it resonated his drum beat back to me, I would get lost in the song and drift off into the dream.

When you experience profound loss in whatever form it comes to you, in that shock and sadness, you may want to just crawl under the covers and stay there, to withdraw from life. I did just that until my daughter said, "Mom, I'm not leaving until you get up, get dressed and feed yourself!" What choice did I have? She had to go back to Colorado and to her own life.

The drum became a sacred tool for my recovery, my own very personal walk with such a harsh teacher, Grief. For me, drumming became the spiritual made physical by sound and motion. It is how I began communicating in a way that went beyond the verbal and touched those hurting places deep within. It was my form of prayer and my connection to the Divine for inspiration and support. It became the gateway I used to find solace and strength, relief from anger and courage in the face of fear; to find my way back to love. The single heartbeat of a drum could bring my body, mind, and spirit together in harmony and balance with a healing vibration that reached my very soul. Ryan gave me the drum beat and its song.

As the darkness of anger, grief or frustration passes through your decision to go on – and trust me, this is a conscious decision you will have to make when you are at any down place in your life. Where do you go from there? I found a way by delving deep into the teachings I was inhaling from the variety of spiritual and practical teachers I had been working with.

Here is an exercise that has proven to be a very useful experience when stress tries to bury me under its heavy blanket. I settle into a warm tub and sink into the gentle arms of the water allowing it to cover me with unconditional support. I sink in until the water covers my ears, and in that underwater silence, I listen to my own heartbeat resonate through the water and back to me. I begin to match the beat of my heart by tapping my fingers on my sternum (breastbone) and listen to the reverberation of my own sacred beat in unison with my heartbeat. My whole body will begin to relax.

Humming Ryan's song, added to the "drumbeats," creates a magical music that feeds my soul and reconnects me with that essence of me that is stronger than the me that sits on any shelf. This "me" that sings back, is the one who jumps from the top shelf in wild abandon and welcomes the day's challenges.

It is the wild-spirited, unstoppable me that can take on the world and make music out of the misery that tries to pull the ladder away from the bookshelf stranding me up there. There is a power in the sound of your heart that carries all possibilities. It is the beat of your life; your soul matching the tempo of the Divine.

What I know through this study and my own personal experience, is that consciously living is all about connecting to that divine source of wisdom, joy, and beauty that is within absolutely every one of us. When we pull together all the pieces of ourselves, we form a new sacred being. That's what I was learning to do; to bring those lost and forgotten parts together into a new wholeness, into the space of where I wanted to be, into who I was becoming.

When we bring our stories into physical form, they are a constant reminder that we have the power to change, create, transform and enliven them every single day. You wind a story into the ties that pull a drum face onto its frame and that drum tells your story every time it is played. You weave your story into a basket and retell it in the design and decoration of each person who admires your creation.

You paint a story as artists have for eons of time, and that painting retells your story each time it is seen.

In those times of sadness and grief, the shadow dwellers and negativity are telling you that it's time to get out of the story you are in. Maybe it's just time to find that piece of your story you have not yet discovered and begin to live it – intentionally, lovingly, fueled by the fire of your soul's own desire. You can change your life if you decide to change your story.

If you like to write and are drawn to drums and drumming, try this exercise that my friend Kate suggested to me years ago. She recommended this as a way for me to connect with myself as I rode the rolling waves of grief. Bring a journal or notepad and pencil or pen. Sit in a quiet place with your drum and clear your mind… Begin drumming and let go of what is all around you. Tap into what is going on inside of you at that moment.

Listen, feel and then write. Write what the drum tells you; the story of you right then, at that moment as you listen to your own heartbeat resonating back to you from the drum. Write what you are feeling from deep within the heartbeat of the drum. Write with the resonance of the moment that you connect with the Divine within you.

I discovered that my story had power when I shared it. Your story has power too! Share it, especially if it is heavy. Allow someone else to help you carry it. The gift of your story may lead them to an eye-opening "aha" moment that changes the direction of their own story.

It is your time to move towards your authentic self and find the voice of your truth in service to your own well-being for the greater good of us all. Get off the shelf, live large and share your stories; inspire those around you to share theirs.

The Universe is conspiring on your behalf to get your story out there. You are the messenger. Take out your key and open the doors to your own loving intentionality and live! Accept that you are a voice of the Divine. Share your hopes and fears, your pain and joy. You are sharing a gift of wisdom, the gift of a life being lived truthfully.

Get off the Shelf, consciously dream your story into existence and share it. Most of all and always, tell your loved ones you love them every time you get the chance and love them with everything you have. Tomorrow isn't guaranteed.

I know sometimes it may seem like "love you... love you too" is just a platitude at the end of a phone call, or hollered out the door as someone leaves. But can you imagine the power of those little words if they were the last ones you ever heard from someone, or even more if they are the last words you ever get the chance to say to them?

There is such power in these words when spoken from the heart. Use them wisely, frequently and with abandon.

Vicki Dobbs

Love Revolution

Love Revolution

Meet the Author

Mia Saenz

Los Angeles, California, USA

Mia Saenz is a Love Advocate and Activist. Her journey into inner personal healing work has catapulted the Love Revolution self-love movement. Mia is a self-love teacher and coach inspiring others to claim their own self-love awareness.

Through her work, Mia has discovered the depth of love on all levels. Love truly is the element most people don't understand and yet it has been there the entire time. Working through love changes the energy of one's story and opens up life to a natural flow. Mia works with people whose desire is to grow their life from trauma, dysfunction, and instability in a powerful stable existence. She teaches a solid path to build a concrete foundation in life. Mia teaches "Love Mastery," and the "Spiritual Elite."

In addition, Mia is also a media host of radio and online TV and is the Founder and Editor-in-Chief of BellaMia magazine, a transformational and holistic lifestyle magazine.

miasaenz.com

bellamiamag.com

Facebook.com/MiaSaenzIStandForLove

Instagram.com/Mia.Saenz.Official

Meet Our Contributing Writers

Barry Selby

Los Angeles, California, USA

Barry Selby is the real deal relationship attraction expert helping strong successful women create balance in love, life, and business.

He is a passionate champion for the divine feminine, and his heart is dedicated to serving women owning their magnificence and authentic power in life as well as in a relationship.

Barry helps amazing women heal their hearts, own their self-love and magnificence, and embrace their feminine majesty, so they become a powerful and positive force in the world and attract their true divine masculine partnership in a relationship.

Learning from his own relationship challenges (of which he definitely had a few), Barry immersed himself in finding out why, and what to do differently. This led him to understand what makes people tick when it comes to matters of the heart.

With over 30 years of study of personal development, interpersonal relationships, spiritual exploration and an embodied understanding of the polarity dance of masculine and feminine, he has refined and matured his own synthesis of skills to help women break the cycle of failed relationships and heartbreak, so they can attract their true divine partnership.

His well-stocked toolbox is specially dedicated to helping you get the love you deserve. Along the way he earned a Master Of Arts in Spiritual Psychology, and is also licensed as a Professional Spiritual Counselor since 2000.

His #1 best-selling first book, 50 Ways To Love Your Lover, helps both singles and couples embrace and embody powerful principles for passionate and richly rewarding relationships.

He is an in-demand inspirational speaker standing for love, healthy romance, and deeply passionate relationship. He brings deep compassion, gentle masculine presence, and wise guidance to assist his clients in their journey to true love.

He has a client base and audience both nationwide and internationally and he loves helping them heal their hearts and honoring themselves.

As one grateful client wrote:

"Barry epitomizes the perfect blend of practical, spiritual, tangible and the intangible in relation to coaching. He comes from a gentle, loving, and friendly spirit that really speaks to women and allowed me to open up to him in a way as if I've known him forever."

barryselby.com

Facebook.com/barryselby.author

Twitter.com/barryselby

Instagram.com/barryselby

YouTube.com/user/barryselby

LinkedIn.com/in/barryselby

itunes.apple.com/us/podcast/messages-from-the-masculine/id1405807132

Rebecka Eggers

San Cristóbal de Las Casas,
Chiapas, Mexico

Rebecka Eggers, The Dream Midwife™ is a Meditation Improv Artist; the creator of the FLARE Brand Storytelling Method™; the author of *Coming Alive!: Spirituality, Activism, & Living Passionately in the Age of Global Domination*; and the creator of Dream Alchemy, The Revelation Story™, a Breathtakingly Beautiful Dream Realization Adventure. She lives in the mountainous highlands of Mexico, where she uses the tools of modern communication to make all kinds of trouble for every last stagnant, soul-killing enemy of your potential. Rebecka helps you bring your dreams to life. She is trained as a Metaphysical Minister, a Co-Active Life Coach, a Reiki Master, and a tax lawyer (probably weren't expecting that last part, eh?). Finally, Rebecka holds a certificate in Digital Marketing through Emeritus and Columbia University, awarded with distinction in 2017.

thepassionpath.vision
Facebook.com/rebeckaeggersandthepassionpath
Twitter.com/Rebecka_Eggers

Kimberley Heart

Los Angeles, California, USA

Love is the new currency of innovative success in life. Kimberley Heart, "the truth teller" has been recognized for over three decades as a thought leader on heart motivated success. The author of two award-winning books, Kimberley Heart has successfully served as a premier keynote speaker, hosted coast to coast radio talk shows, and is a strategic consultant to Fortune 500 companies, nationally ranked law firms and their leaders. Her practical, proven strategies have worked for an organization like yours inspiring a higher quality of life and improving the bottom-line.

Kimberley Heart's unprecedented strategic advantage is knowing how to utilize heart-based thinking to merge the powers of intellect, passion, and imagination. She has pioneered new approaches to leadership utilizing the 7 words never used in business but guaranteed to bring success. An innovator in both her approach and her delivery, Kimberley has a clear understanding of what truly motivates us.

kimberleyheart.com

Debbie Murad

Los Angeles, California, USA

L. Debbie Murad, LCSW, is a Professor at the USC School of Social Work. She often serves as a clinical consultant for social service agencies in the Los Angeles area. Her areas of expertise include trauma, domestic abuse, addiction, and human development and behavior.

Debbie Murad is an active member of the social justice focused Southern California Women's Council with NASW. Her expertise includes trauma and co-occurring substance abuse and mental health issues.

Ms. Murad has over a 25 year history in the domestic violence movement. Her professional experience includes addiction treatment, creating and managing domestic violence programs, and developing and implementing unique services. She has a psychotherapy and life coach Private Practice.

She is an avid hiker and meditator and offers alternative therapies, including nature and yoga based therapies for peace and balance. Her latest endeavor is the natural Balance Program, which promotes mental, physical and spiritual health and wellbeing.

debbiemuradmsw.com

Facebook.com/debbie.murad.5

Instagram.com/DebbieMurad

Christina Sharp

Chelmsford, United Kingdom

Christina Sharp is a Spiritual Life and Mindset coach with particular interest and experience in the spheres of Midlife Transition and Faith/Spirituality.

She works with her clients and online community to create lives that are aligned in all areas with who each individual really is, in their souls' essence. Seeing where they are stuck in lies or limiting beliefs, and uncovering their deep values, she walks alongside others as they cultivate their own Self-Trust and Faith in the Divine. This process creates the freedom to face and manage the inevitable changes life brings and to live on purpose, in serenity, and with joy.

Christina experienced a deep transition in her own life when she freed herself from an emotionally painful marriage, only to face disapproval and abandonment of her faith community. She had a choice – to return to her marriage and silence her aching soul or to find the courage to walk her own path, wherever it might lead. She chose the latter.

She now knows that path leads to the blessings only a truly connected, Self-Aligned Life can bring.

Love Revolution

Christina has over 20 years' experience guiding women along with their faith journey, both in groups and as individuals. She now couples that experience with a passion to lead people into their own deep truth and authentic self-expression.

She believes a peaceful and purposeful existence comes from the Life Alignment of three key areas essential to our growth and fulfilment:

Connection to God/Spirit

Trust of Self

Self-Expressive Relationship with the World

Christina has experienced many life transitions of her own.

She was born in Sydney, Australia, to English parents and moved to the UK in her early twenties. She ministered alongside her then-husband in various churches prior to her divorce after 20 years of marriage.

She worked in banking before returning to her love of serving and spiritually supporting others, this time through her coaching practice.

Christina is now very happily remarried and living in the English countryside.

She is currently transitioning into the empty nest stage of life as her two daughters step out into their own adult lives.

christinasharpcoaching.com/
Facebook.com/christinasharpcoaching
Instagram.com/christina.sharp

Carla M. Jones

Dublin, Ireland

Reveal the powerful you. As a published author, speaker, and purpose-driven coach, Carla M. Jones helps people understand who they are, and their life's purpose, so that they can intentionally create a life with meaning and abundant success. Fascinated and deeply interested in the associations between behavior, personal beliefs systems, and fulfillment, Carla spends her time learning and researching different techniques, psychologies, mindfulness and other approaches to success. She helps her clients to get clear on what they want and how to get it, in a way that is true and unique to who they are.

One of Carla's foundational beliefs is that we are wholly responsible for every experience in our life and that everything that happens, happens for us - as a gift to our future selves. Carla's clients come to use their fears, past traumas and circumstances in life as fuel to find their inner purpose and learn to accept themselves, and the world around them, with more depth and unconditional love.

Carla runs a successful global coaching practice from Dublin, Ireland. Her coaching allows her clients in achieving balanced fulfillment and success in Business, Relationships, Health and Life.

Carla has a no-excuses approach to coaching that is very hands-on. She empowers her clients to imagine the possibilities and see the opportunities at each moment. A strong focus on healthy sustainability, a resourceful mindset, and a strategic structure give her clients a safe-space to explore their goals and dreams, to listen to and trust their inner voice, and find the best way to create the life they were born to live. Whether her clients are seeking coaching in their careers or their personal lives, Carla's extensive training and diplomas in various fields, along with over 3500 hours of one-to-one coaching experience gives Carla an edge in her ability to move people from where they are to where they want to be.

Her first book looks at nutrition, lifestyle, and happiness. Her next book will help her readers reveal the guru that lives within each of us. She coaches, teaches, and speaks on personal development around the world in English, French, Portuguese and Spanish.

carlamjones.com

Facebook.com/CarlaMJonesCoach

Instagram.com/carlamjonescoach

LinkedIn.com/in/carlamjones

Twitter.com/carlamjones

Jodi Polen

Chicago, Illinois, USA

Jodi Polen has helped hundreds of clients to awaken to self-love and self-actualization by teaching co-creation, manifestation, and skills for higher vibration. Her work includes relief from pain and illness with the healing of mental, emotional and spiritual issues. She is three-time recipient of The Highland Park Business Hall of Fame Alternative and Holistic Health Award. Jodi's business is called, "FLOW Energy Healing."

Jodi Polen is an accomplished Reiki Master Teacher, Clairvoyant, and Medium. She uses a combination of crystals, essential oils, singing crystal bowls, drumming, divination tools and entity removal in her work. She accesses the Akashic Records for those seeking the history of their souls. As an empath, Jodi communicates with departed loved ones and is an open master channel. She uses Reiki along with the knowledge and energies from other modalities of healing to create amazing transformation in people's lives for their overall health and well-being. Jodi Polen has been interviewed on national radio shows.

Jodi currently resides in Deerfield, IL with her husband, two beautiful daughters, one dog and two cats.

What sets Jodi apart are the struggles she's learned from on her own path to self-enlightenment and the knowledge she's gained throughout her journey that she can share with her clients. Her heart-centered approach touches each individual at their core, creating an undeniable energy unique to her – where personal transformation is attainable and inevitable.

Jodi Polen's mission in life is to heal the world teaching self-love, opening new consciousness and self-actualization one person at a time.

flowenergyhealing.com

jodipolen.com

Facebook.com/flowenergyhealing

Instagram.com/jodipolen

Patty Alfonso

Los Angeles, California, USA

Patty Alfonso is a Leader. Speaker. Author.

A catalyst for transformation, Patty Alfonso is an internationally acclaimed speaker and facilitator on the topics of consciousness, bodies and creating a life that inspires global change. She has spoken on international stages in front of royalty and government officials as well as thought leaders and influencers from all over the world.

The author of #1 International Best Selling books *Your Body as the Creation of Consciousness* and *Dancing as the Body of Consciousness*, Patty is also the host of the weekly show *Consciousness is Sexy* where she re-defines *sexy* as a way of being in the world with more consciousness and vulnerability.

Patty is the creator of Pole Dancing for Consciousness™ and The Essence of You™. Her signature programs have invited her clients to have more ease, joy, pleasure, and communion with their bodies. Exploring intimacy with Self, her kind and witty facilitation inspire her clients to melt away their limitations and open the door to new possibilities in their life with their bodies, businesses and relationships.

Patty received her Bachelor's Degree in Sociology from Emory University. She is certified as a Body/Mind Counselor and an Energy Healing Therapist. Patty's desire to continue growing and empower her clients led her to the tools of Access Consciousness®, where she is a Certified Facilitator.

A global traveler and facilitator, Patty currently resides in Los Angeles where she enjoys horseback riding, going to the movies, lounging by the pool, reading and creating her business with ease, joy, and glory!

For more information about Patty's creations go to:

PattyAlfonso.Sexy
Consciousness.Sexy
YourBodyIsConsciousness.com
PoleDancingForConsciousness.com
DancingAsTheBodyOfConsciousness.com

Dana Canneto

Westchester, New York, USA

Dana Canneto is both a
Transformational Guide and
Embodiment Coach whose specialty
is working with sensitive and empathic women. Through her work as
founder of Body Divinity™ and Revival Dance™, Dana teaches
body-centered awareness as the gateway to access inner power.

Throughout this process, women learn how to re-connect to the
sacred wisdom of their bodies and are left empowered to know and
trust their own inner truth, embrace their unique gifts, and claim
their true power.

Dana uses a variety of healing modalities including somatic healing,
energy work, body movement, and intuitive offerings and guidance.
She is certified as a Reiki Practitioner, Holistic Health Coach, Life
Coach and Practitioner of the Magical Awakenings® healing system
and is deeply committed to creating space for women to come home
to themselves in body, mind, and spirit. This soul transformative
work supports them in creating more freedom, joy, and purpose in
their lives.

Through her experience gained in education as well as through her own personal healing journey, she is able to powerfully and effectively share her gifts in transformative ways with women all over the world.

danacanneto.com
Facebook.com/danacanneto
Facebook.com/groups/bodydivinitytribe
Instagram.com/bodydivinity

Stori Nagel

Los Angeles, California, USA

Stori Nagel grew up with illness on both sides of her family. Multiple Sclerosis was diagnosed in her mother when she was just 31, Stori was only eight. Then at twelve, her father's cousin informed her of hereditary breast cancer in the family. She just had this feeling that traumatic illness of some kind was always stalking her. She tried to make the most out of the time she felt she had, before she got sick.

When Stori was diagnosed with breast cancer at 38, it really wasn't a surprise. As a result of her experiences, she and her husband founded Haus of Volta, a nonprofit aimed at bringing self-love and mindfulness to young breast cancer survivors worldwide. As a medical "outlier" (someone who does not respond well to pharmaceutical medication) she has sought out alternative pain, stress and depression management.

Self-imposed starvation, due to body dysmorphia, in her early 30s left her with adrenal fatigue and electromagnetic hypersensitivity. Seeing and feeling low-frequency electrical waves has taken years of adjustment and understanding to comprehend and manage. Her childhood dreams of seeing, feeling and hearing things beyond generalized comprehension have come to fruition.

Stori's sincere wish is that you find your heart light. She hopes this book will support that in your life.

hausofvolta.com

Christine Miskinis

Middletown, New Jersey, USA

Christine Miskinis is a Feminine Power Coach who focuses on teaching women how to tune in to their inner voice to express their Authentic Voice in their lives. She is the owner and founder of Rock it Out Woman.

Christine's story began with healing her own voice when she found out at age 24 that she had pre-cancerous cells growing from her stomach up into her esophagus from a lifetime of digestive issues. She believes this was a direct result of not listening to her intuition, pushing her way through life and silencing her own Voice in trying to be a successful woman. It wasn't until that moment in the Doctor's office that she realized no one was going to save her, there was no magic pill to fix her, and that she was responsible for her life - Body, Mind, and Spirit.

In fact, she recalls everything around her going completely silent as she heard her inner voice say, "Go and allow your body to Heal." Trusting her inner voice, she left the office unafraid and within a few days the perfect mentor showed up to support her in her healing process. The more her physical body healed, the greater her VOICE inside became. In just 6 months, her body was healed. From there,

Christine went on to discover many more truths of the world, and was ignited with passion for her newly discovered purpose to support other women in tuning in to their own inner voice, for the guidance needed to transform their lives.

As she began sharing her story, she quickly became noticed in the Coaching industry and soon others were asking her to tell her story of healing to their audiences. Christine has been seen multiple times on National Television (Dr. Oz), FOX5 NY and she hosts her own weekly Radio Show as a VOICE for women on spreaker.com called Rock it Out Radio: http://www.spreaker.com/show/rock-it-out-radio-with-christine! Christine hosted her first LIVE Event this year, "Rock your VOICE, Woman LIVE" in NYC with keynote speaker, Marianne Williamson!

"Everything I need to be successful happens through the Power of my Voice, both Inner-connection and Outer expression. I believe the power of a woman is found in her Voice." – Christine

rockitoutwoman.com
Facebook.com/rockitoutwoman
Instagram.com/rockitoutwoman

Susan Kokura

Manhattan, New York, USA

Dr. Susan Kokura, PharmD is a
corporate Clinical Pharmacy
Manager in Pharmacy Informatics
for NewYork-Presbyterian Health system in Manhattan. She is a
south Indian born, New York City-based author, poet, pharmacist
and mother to two boys. Susan is an avid international foodie and
cook, is a whiz at whipping up delicious cocktails (thanks to a
bartending degree she got in college), and enjoys writing poetry in
addition to her other writing projects. A kid at heart, don't be
surprised to see her playing with her sons' toys and games more than
they do. She has been published in numerous medical journals and is
an ongoing contributor to various publications.

Susan was born in Kerala, India and raised there until the age of 8
when she emigrated with her family to America. Susan, seeing the
lack of south Asian cultural diversity in children's books decided to
create her own and write the book series available on Amazon called
The Adventures of Molz. She developed Molz based on her
childhood memories to represent her own heritage and the diversity
of South Indian culture.

She received her doctorate of pharmacy degree from the University of Sciences in Philadelphia and has been practicing in different areas of pharmacy for 13 years. She resides in New York with her family and works toward promoting literacy all over the state by volunteering as a writing coach, reading her own books and other pieces of writing, building books etc. in different underserved student populations and schools around the state.

Susan.kokura@gmail.com

Whitney Freya

Wallowa, Oregon, USA

Whitney Freya is a creative visionary who knows that when you consciously create your reality from love, your wildest desires become your truth. She is the published author of three books on personal creativity, including her latest, *Rise Above, Free Your Mind One Brush Stroke at a Time.*

Her unique approach to personal creativity and her personal journey from a wanna-be artist to where she is today has garnered her international media attention. She leads her online Creatively Fit Coach Certification so others can share her passion and create money energy by teaching her Sacred Personal Painting Practice. Whitney Freya has been a featured speaker worldwide at locations like The Esalen Institute, Burning Man, Awesomeness Fest, and at Agape Spiritual Center. She lives in the mountains in NE Oregon and holds retreats there in the summers. Learn more and join the Life Artist "palette".

whitneyfreya.com

Michelle Mor

Pasadena, California, USA

In a quest for inner peace I began my journey of self-discovery. In that process, I uncovered what has become my life's work. This began as a teenager, when my mother would take me to Real Estate seminars, which was essentially a coaching environment.

I have been a hairstylist for 35 years, where I have often been coaching my clients! I have 13 years of professional coaching experience and I'm continually growing personally so that I can become a better coach. I believe with all my heart that there is no greater gift than to stand for someone in transformation—to be a part of a life that has been altered forever because they trusted me to support them on their journey.

Love and acceptance bring freedom into a relationship, and the greatest gift is to watch their lives come together when they find their voices after a long struggle. I am so grateful that I have the privilege to make a difference in the world doing what I love.

MichelleMor.com

Patricia Daly

Markethill, Co Armagh, Northern
Ireland

In 2015, Patricia Daly founded
"Self-Transformation Through
Music" as a means of transforming women's lives through online
coaching. It wasn't long before Patricia discovered a specific niche
in finding inner peace in life. Patricia's self-transformation through
music evolved into "The Spiritually Fulfilled Woman," a personal
transformation coaching service providing happiness, freedom and
inner peace: fulfilling a deep spiritual connection to life force energy
flow. Patricia works directly with smart, professional, middle-aged
women.

Honored with an M.A. in Music Performance, Artist Awards from
the Arts Council of Northern Ireland and holder of the Senior All-
Ireland Harpist title, with a reputation that goes well beyond
Ireland's shores, Patricia Daly, is primarily known as a personal
transformation coach, mentor and an accomplished performing artist
displaying skills acquired through years of research, performance
and her own personal life journey!

self-transformationthroughmusic.com

Bonnie Gayle

Beverly Hills, California, USA

Bonnie Gayle, Body Liberator, educates, speaks, and writes on how to feel comfortable and confident in your body, connect intimately and step into your personal, sensual power. Bonnie's past life experience includes negative body image, bulimia and compulsive overeating, low self-esteem, being stalked and raped. These traumatic experiences combined with self-loathing and coping in unhealthy ways, led to withdrawal, binging and purging, emotional eating, promiscuity, and self-deprecation. After healing her negative body image and lack of self-worth, Bonnie has successfully assisted, mentored, and educated both men and women on the importance of appreciating, enjoying, and loving their bodies. "Daily pleasure, self-care, loving yourself, and your body promotes living a successful vibrant life." Bonnie Gayle

BodyResetForWomen.com
BonnieGayle.com
Facebook.com/BonnieGayle1
Twitter.com/theBonnieGayle
Instagram.com/thebonniegayle

Love Revolution

Kellie Valenti
Lima, Ohio, USA

Kellie Valenti is a Holistic Wellness Mentor. When people are unhealthy and feel hopeless that's when tragedy most often occurs. In a society of instant gratification, we often tend to overlook how to heal our own bodies. My great passion is to help individuals and families learn the basics of health by building a strong foundation through their gut.

I know that there aren't one-size fits all approaches to health. That's why my background in fermentation and traditional nutrient-dense whole food activism plays an integral part in the holistic gut health healing process.

When I was a young girl growing up in Ohio, my parents always gardened. Sometimes they raised pasture-fed animals and practiced the art of fermentation. I didn't always understand what this meant in terms of health and family, but now I do. I have a deep appreciation for the foundation it provided for me in my life. My early years formed a foundation that wrapped around wellness for most of my life. I always innately understood the importance of good health, exercise and the love of good food.

Love Revolution

As a young adult, my experimentation with sourdough began. I had an infatuation with great bread(s) and sharing them with everyone that would take them. When my children were growing up, meal time was an important part of family time. The family table was a place of community, good food, and love. It was a place for sharing and dreaming.

With a background in the wellness industry for almost half of my adult life, I have helped people realize their true potential, gain confidence, look and feel their best and ultimately win better health. It made sense to resurrect my love of fermentation and healing foods, such as sourdough and nourishing broths. Now I get to help others in their healing journey and share the passion I have for quality, nutrient-dense nutrition.

I love teaching others about the possibility that lies in each of us to heal our own bodies from sickness and disease. It empowers you to be a proactive participant in your own health, your family's too. Why settle for a life of mediocrity when you can have a life of abundance and vitality, Naturally!

A health blog writer, a connoisseur of cookbooks, lover of recipes, music, good wine and co-host of the Kellie and Sara Show, I invite you to take the first step on a journey, where hope, health, and healing begin.

livelifeyearsyounger.com

Facebook.com/LiveLifeYearsYounger

Sharon Otness

Seattle, Washington, USA

Sharon Otness, Founder, and CEO of Design Your Beautiful Life is a certified holistic health counselor living in Seattle, WA. She is the Health & Wellness Content Director for Unlimited Woman Magazine, Lifestyle Director for BellaMia Magazine, and was a former Featured Writer for I Am Enough Magazine. She is also a licensed Desire Map facilitator, Yoga Instructor, and an Essential Oils Educator. She creates custom malas as Sacred Adornment. Her holistic approach to emotional health and wellness allows her to help women of all ages meet the challenges of food, ultimate vitality, and aging gracefully in a fast-paced world. Sharon is passionate about supporting clients through depression, anxiety, and life transitions so they can discover the balanced and amazing life they were meant to live, full of meaning, love and without self-deprivation or guilt.

sharonotness.com

Facebook.com/healthylifestylecoach

Claire Geddes
Washington, D.C., USA

Claire Geddes is a writer, part-time comedian and student of mind-body modalities. She has taken a long road to recover her health, both mind and body.

Traditional medicine and therapy only led her in circles, on medication, and talking incessantly about the problems rather than solutions. Part of that journey has involved growing stronger in her own convictions and paying less attention to others' thoughts about what to do and believe.

She is fascinated by the subconscious and convinced that the answers lie deep inside all of us. This was the idea behind her children's book, Finley the Flute.

Claire has an MBA and a master's degree in arts management. After finding her career unfulfilling, she wondered why most people do things they really don't want to do. Depression led her to ask: "is this really the way life is supposed to be?"

The questions kept coming and led her to become fascinated with how we are "programmed" and how to "unprogram" ourselves to find out what truly lights us up. The answer for her was to help others find that out for themselves and laugh about it along the way.

clairegeddes.com/

Karen Tax

Durham, North Carolina, USA

Karen Tax is the Executive
Leadership Coach and Culture
Change Consultant. She is a speaker
and author who coaches people to discover their genius so they can
be happy, influential and successful at work. She specializes in
creating success without sacrifice, compromise, or struggle, where
everyone wins, all voices are heard, and Love rules.

Karen creates these audacious results using a proprietary system
called the IAM Way. It is a 5 step holistic (head, spirit, heart, body)
leadership and career development approach that guides people to
discover their passions, authentic self, and personal power, so they
can lead and succeed based on their own definition of success.

This exact same system is also used in her business consulting to
create genius cultures, that rely less on external structures of
compliance and control and more on leadership at all levels. The
brilliant energy of the people in your organization is leveraged and
recognized to create higher profits, more engagement, and
sustainable growth.

Karen started her career as a Software Engineer. Frustration with her work environment, and her inability to influence inspired her to get a master's degree in Organization Development from a highly esteemed program that evolved out of the German Holocaust. It's a field that was started by Kurt Lewin, a psychologist dedicated to understanding why good people sit by and let bad things happen to others.

Karen became deeply committed to creating change that would end the oppression of all kinds – especially in the workplace. Karen wanted to find out how to create companies that were successful, profitable, and streamlined, without causing harm to employees or the planet. The IAM Way emerged as a balanced, reliable and honest approach for everyone to be happy, passionately engaged, and authentically brilliant at work.

Karen was heavily influenced by 7 years working at Nortel Networks, a business that had 100,000 employees worldwide and went from $30 billion in sales to crushing bankruptcy. From that experience, Karen saw firsthand how fear erodes trust. Even using the most current best practices in change management, the change agents at Nortel weren't able to save this company from self-destruction. Karen learned there that the very best academic research and approaches were too slow, too complicated, and too analytical to actually be effective.

Karen's insatiable quest for the holy grail of transformation led her to confront her own deepest, darkest demons, and professionally to explore the nether reaches of "woo woo" where no software engineer would imagine finding herself. Karen learned critical soft skills and translated them to be practical in the workplace. She developed the IAM Way over time, based in her academic training, corporate experience, deep personal transformation, and confirmed results.

The core of what Karen learned is that there is one key step that must happen before all others if we are to create happy and healthy work experiences that benefit everyone involved. That key step is to shift from a mindset of fear and scarcity to a mindset of Love and abundance.

theiamway.com

Geoff Laughton

Boulder, Colorado, USA

Geoff Laughton, an internationally in-demand Relationship Coach and Expert, known as Your Relationship Architect, is also the author of the internationally best-selling books, "Instant Insights on Building a Conflict-Proof Relationship" and "Built to Last: Designing & Maintaining a Loving, Lasting, and Passionate Relationship." For the last 21 years, he's been guiding couples and individuals in designing and building the conscious, Spirit-led relationships and life they truly desire. He is also the CEO and lead facilitator of The Evolving Man Men's Community.

Far too many people settle for what they believe is just the best they can hope to get. Geoff is devoted to guiding and mentoring people in how to have love relationships and lives that go beyond settling to instead create truly expansive, harmonious connections that heal and expedite the dreams that people have simply neglected and/or forgotten over time. A great amount of what Geoff teaches and guides people through has come from Geoff's own adventures in his marriage of 36 years.

To date, Geoff has worked with thousands of private clients and couples; has led over 300 workshops around the country for singles and couples, and has spoken at numerous live and online events.

yourrelationshiparchitect.com
Facebook.com/buildyourdreamrelationship
Twitter.com/geofflaughton
Linkedin.com/in/geofflaughton

Antia and Broderick Boyd

San Diego, California, USA

Antia and Broderick Boyd have
helped thousands of elite single men
and women around the world. Antia
studied Personality Psychology at UC Berkeley. Broderick has a
degree in Communications and Interpersonal Relationships. They
have been keynote speakers at such places as Harvard University and
Google. For a couple of decades combined they've studied
everything that they could get their hands on in the areas of
communication, love and eliminating fear in relationships. They live
in San Diego, California.

Findtheoneelite.com

Facebook.com/AntiaAndBrodyBoyd

Dr. Sharon Cohen

Newport Beach, California, USA

Dr. Sharon Cohen, Relationship &
Love Consultant, works with
women who can't seem to find the
right relationship or who aren't sure they're in the right relationship.

Many of her clients are successful at work and in every other area of
their life but struggle to have romantic relationships work.

She helps her clients have committed, deeply loving relationships.

Knowing that you are so worthy of healthy, beautiful, stable, JUICY
love is what lights Dr. Sharon up. She is certain that having love in
your life is possible for you.

Even if you've lost hope, she will hold the space of hope for you.

With 25 years of experience in the field and seven years specifically
focused on dating, love, communication, and relationship issues, Dr.
Sharon's commitment is to help women like you have the
relationship of your dreams by helping you to blossom open to
receive ever-lasting love.

Currently, Dr. Sharon works as a consultant from the philosophy that what her clients want and need are expertise, objectivity, strategy, a catalyst for change, and a teacher. She trains you how to be the best, most self-loving you and what to say or do that is in the highest and best use for you.

The work she does with her clients rewires their brains so that changes made last a lifetime.

What sets Dr. Sharon apart from others is that her work stems from the aggregate of her background as a psychotherapist, as a student of Dr. Pat Allen, Carl Jung, transactional analysis, the sciences of child and adult attachment, biology, brain, and body science, her personal journey, and her continued thirst for on-going knowledge.

A native of Newport Beach, California, Dr. Sharon graduated from UCLA and received her Master in Social Work from the University of Southern California. She received her Doctor of Philosophy from the University of Texas at Austin, School of Social Work. She has an extensive background working in the psychiatric hospital setting with addictions and mental health issues.

A few fun facts about Dr. Sharon:

- Sharon volunteered for Austin's South by Southwest as the Film Festival Party coordinator for seven years, welcoming in VIPs and guests at the door of up to 25 parties per year.

- After a lifetime of considering herself a "non-runner," Sharon completed a half-marathon a few years ago.

- Sharon and her husband rescued a 7-year old dog from death row. Sparky the wonder dog is now living a cushy life in their loving home.

- Along with thousands of others, Sharon attended the one and possibly only "Desert Trip" Rock Concert featuring the Rolling Stones, The Who, Neil Young, Paul McCartney, Bob Dylan, and Roger Waters of Pink Floyd.

At this time, Dr. Sharon sees clients in her Newport Beach office and via phone consultation for people who live across the country or internationally.

drsharoncohen.com
Facebook.com/drsharoncohen
Twitter.com/drsharon
Instagram.com/drsharoncohen
Youtube.com/user/drsharoncohen

Kim Louise Morrison

London, Ontario, Canada

Kim Louise Morrison is a #1 international bestselling author, an intuitive empowerment coach, a motivational speaker, and a practitioner of several energetic healing modalities. She's also a certified Access Consciousness Bars® Facilitator.

As an empowerment coach and recovered "supreme self-judger" Kim Louise Morrison understands the self-confidence struggle. It's her business and her passion to guide people to release the self-judgment that stops them from thriving and embrace dynamic self-empowerment, so they have the confidence to go after their dreams.

She has an active coaching, healing, teaching and speaking business.

She has been featured on the Writing on Air and Unchained With Becky Herdt radio shows, as well as a featured guest on The Erica Glessing Show podcast.

Kim currently lives in London, Ontario Canada.

kimlouisemorrison.com

Amazon.com: From Black and White to Technicolor

Facebook.com/kimlouisemorrison

Vicki Dobbs

Clovis, California, USA

Vicki Dobbs is an Author, Teacher, Counselor, Coach: A Connoisseur of Creativity

Vicki is a subtle warrior walking a path of heart to manifest spirituality in everyday lives, She opens existential gateways for individuals to face their challenges and embrace them as the great teachers they are. Her goal is to see everyone walk in beauty and balance every day of their lives, empowered by the voice of their own authentic truth.

Through Sacred Wisdom Workshops, Vicki creates opportunities for others to make deep personal changes through experiential classes, ceremony, and story. She endeavors to inspire others to create their lives intentionally. Vicki is an Inspirator of everyday awareness, an Instigator of spontaneous stories and a Connoisseur of Creativity. Gratitude and grace sprinkled with humility and humor are the medicine she brings to the world.

The human spirit inside each of us has an enormous capacity to survive through every unexpected twist and turn life has to offer. As an elder, teacher, and entrepreneur, a spiritual coach and ordained minister and as a crafter of sacred art and tools, Vicki perceives life's journey as an ever-upward spiraling ascension of the human spirit bringing her wisdom, wholeness, and authenticity.

When you connect with your own truth, that authentic voice inside that says YES, you touch the Divine within you that sparks your passion, ignites your joy and takes you to new levels of living. That is the essence of what Vicki brings to her classes and workshops, her online programs and her stories.

Please visit her website for a special gift and join her Facebook community for updated information on art, journals, projects, and workshops currently available.

vickidobbs.com
Facebook.com/SacredWisdomTeachings

Confidence is an inside job!

Natural Balance
Debbie Murad, LCSW

"Happiness is not a matter of intensity but of balance and order
and rhythm and harmony." —Thomas Merton

Are are you in harmony and balance in all areas of
your life?

How do you find balance?

For more guidance, click here to learn about my Natural Balance Plan:

Offerings include individual psychotherapy & intensive concierge therapy.
Individual coaching and personalized coaching plans for body, mind and spiritual
Balance:
  · Self-care plans
  · Meditation
  · Mindfulness — eating, walking living
  · Reflection and contemplation
  · Healthy eating and living

Join me on my *Love Unconditionally* course today. Let go of the past pains and negative thinking and learn to love yourself, others and life unconditionally in just 7 days! All my Love,

Carla M Jones

http://courses.carlamjones.com
carla@carlamjones.com

Have you lost your balance?

Connecting to your energy flow not only feels great, it allows you to up-level your life.

Claim your free copy of Replenish <u>here</u>.
www.jodipolen.com/lovesfreegift

THE
Body LOVE CLUB

AN **INTIMATE** PLAYGROUND
FOR YOU WITH YOUR **BODY**

WITH PATTY ALFONSO

WHAT IF YOU COULD FIND *pleasure* IN EVERYTHING YOU DO JUST FOR YOU?

www.pattyalfonso.sexy/bodyloveclub

When Our Body Awakens
Our Spirit Comes Alive

A Remembering

A Reclaiming

A Revival of your Divine Spirit

Ready to feel the freedom
in being who you are?

Let me show you how!

Body Divinity
www.danacanneto.com

CREATE your own
Love Revolution &
RISE ABOVE!

Join me for my Master Class Series today.

whitneyfreyastudio.com

Ditch the Diets!

Learn a way of eating your body loves...

Lose weight. Feel great.
Decrease inflammation.
And **NEVER** go on a diet again.

https://BodyResetForWomen.com

"If you are constantly on the edge of stress and anxiety, it is time to learn new tools" – Sharon

Feeling Stressed and Overwhelmed?
It's time to get Zen

Your Journey To Zen

yourjourneytozen.com

YOU'VE BEEN CLIMBING UP THAT CORPORATE LADDER FOR A WHILE

"Maybe with *different* decisions, with a *different* tack

things might be different"

OR SO YOU THOUGHT

yet here you are again, in the same toxic place as before

YOUR HEART HURTS *with a crisis of confidence*

your body aches FROM RELENTLESS OVERWHELM

YOU WANT **CHANGE**

and this time, you're ABSOLUTELY CLEAR that it's got to be

FOR REAL

- -

WELL, WELL, WELL. GUESS WHAT? TURNS OUT

happy, healthy, meaningful

and PROFITABLE WORK *is* POSSIBLE

theiamway.com/gift

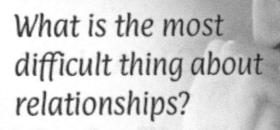

What is the most difficult thing about relationships?

Is fighting disconnecting you both from your love?

It doesn't need to be that way!

Let me show you how...
Grab your copy of my latest
book to get the secret.
(amazon.com/dp/B06Y5N7K7N)

Geoff Laughton
YourRelationshipArchitect.com

What If you had more confidence?

Would you go after your **dreams?**

How would your empowered life look if you had the **3 keys to building confidence** while going after your dreams?

Let me show you!

vickidobbs.com

When was the last time you felt you heart on fire,
heard your soul sing or watched
a buffalo gallop across the sky?

An EVOLUTION OF WISDOM Awaits...

**It is time to RE-MEMBER YOU
and RE-CLAIM Love!**

**Click here for a
Special GIFT**
www.sacredwisdomworkshops.com/workshops/

Made in the USA
Coppell, TX
31 October 2020

40546844R00203